# Choosing Joy
# Creating Abundance:

## Practical Tools for Manifesting your Desires.

ELLEN PETERSON

# DEDICATION

To my beautiful daughters, Kelci, and Marissa, who grew up
learning how to manifest and who are now passionately
following their own dreams.
To Michele, who has added love and laughter to my life
of joy and abundance.

# Table of Contents

Ellen Peterson

# Acknowledgements

I must first thank God for always giving me all that I need to follow my dreams. He is the best co-author that anyone could ever ask for.

I give thanks to my loving family, Michele, Kelci, and Marissa, who provide me with the love and support necessary to make dreams become reality.

I thank my parents, Charles and Doris Peterson, who have taught me a great deal about both prosperity and perseverance.

I want to thank all my family and friends, who touch my heart and teach me about true wealth. I also thank my many clients, past, present, and future, who have allowed me into their lives and who continue to teach me about courage and integrity.

I give thanks to the Wellness Institute for their inspiration and support. And lastly, thank you to my readers who repeatedly remind me how valuable this information is in the journey of life.

Like all matters important to life, we cannot do it alone. May your lives be peaceful, happy, and incredibly prosperous. May each day bring you laughter and may all your dreams come true!

Ellen Peterson

# Introduction

Life is to be enjoyed, not endured.

Life is good. There is so much good in the world and yet we often do not know how to attract it into our lives. When was the last time you genuinely felt happy, content, and fulfilled? When was the last time you said, "I am really happy"? Do you feel that you have everything you could ever possibly ask for or need? If the answer is no, then why not?

Life is so rich with all that you need and want, but most people need to learn how to connect with the unlimited supply of good that exists here on earth. Just as the telephone operator connects you to the call you need, your good awaits you. It is waiting for you to use the necessary channels for connection to your intended good. When that connection occurs, there is a continual flow of positive things in your life.

My personal journey began as I was training for my certification in hypnotherapy through the Wellness Institute. The idea of manifesting good things in life was initially presented to me in an unfamiliar term: prosperity. For the first time, I realized that there might be an easier way to be successful and have all the things I would like to have in my life. Prosperity is a fascinating word, and one that is too often applied to someone other than us.

We consider others to be prosperous, while we struggle to survive. I want this book to introduce you to the joy and prosperity of life. I want it to help you to revive your belief in yourself, your abilities, and your dreams. I want you to recognize that all things are possible and that you do not have to settle for less than having it all. You need to have dreams. Dreams are the avenue through which we achieve success and true prosperity. To be without a dream is to be without a plan. You are then at a loss for what to do. Give yourself permission to dream and to succeed.

The stories and personal accounts within this book reflect the actual experiences of various people. However, their names have been appropriately changed to maintain their anonymity.

This book incorporates information pertaining to spirituality. It is not intended to persuade you to believe in any specific spiritual belief or practice. It does not matter who you believe in as a guiding presence; what matters is that you believe in someone or something that is much greater than the mortal world. It was my hope to take into consideration varied beliefs. However, given the diversity of perceptions regarding spirituality, the terms Higher Power, the Universe, and God are used interchangeably throughout this book.

If this is the beginning of your journey, I hope that you will find it to be exciting and rewarding, and that you will reach your goals, no matter how big or grandiose they seem to you now. I hope that you will choose to push out the walls of reality and look beyond the visible to discover joy in life. Invest in developing a love for life. Invest in doing what you enjoy most. Dare to be prosperous. Dare to live your life fully and happily. Dare to dream in color!

# Chapter 1

## Prosperity: Daring to Dream in Color

Star light, star bright. The first star I see tonight.
I wish I may, I wish I might have the wish I wish tonight.

Whether you wish upon a star or quietly within yourself, you have dreams waiting to come alive. These dreams may include owning your own business, earning a college degree, driving a new vehicle, or building your own home. It does not matter what your dreams consist of if you allow yourself the privilege of dreaming. Dreams inspire a person to accomplish remarkable things.

There are two categories of dreamers in this world: there are those who have dreams, and there are those who actively pursue their dreams. The simple dreamers talk about their dreams and goals but lack the knowledge or capability to accomplish their stated goals. They simply dream for the purpose of dreaming. They lack the confidence required to act toward achieving those dreams.

The simple dreamers often place the arrival of their dreams somewhere outside of themselves. That is, they believe that something or someone will come along and make their dreams come true. They talk of winning the lottery or landing a million-dollar contract someday. And so, they wait. And wait. And wait. Consequently, their dreams remain just that, dreams.

Simple dreamers live in the hope that "someday I will be rich." They become lost in their hopes and paralyzed with fear at the thought of taking any action toward making their dreams a reality. The master dreamers, on the other hand, are those who do whatever it takes to make their dreams a reality. They physically and emotionally push their dreams forward, regardless of obstacles or feelings of discouragement. They actively participate in the process of bringing their dreams into fruition.

Most people are reluctant to take the risks necessary to make their dreams come true. They fear the hurt and disappointment that follows failed dreams. And so, they stay where they are. They simply wait and hope for their dreams to come true and for prosperity to knock at their door. They settle for what they believe to be true rather than what could be true.

Often when we consider the promise of dreams, we think about having and accomplishing important things. We are curious about those people who have somehow found their way to "the good life." This brand of life is eloquently described in magazines and newspapers, with its fancy cars, extravagant homes, and million-dollar careers. The "good life" portrays a life of ease and comfort, in which people have made their dreams come true.

*It is a universal desire to live a happy and content life.*

Every person has at least one dream, but problems arise because people do not permit themselves to believe in their dreams. They minimize or deny themselves their dreams. They convince themselves that their dreams are unrealistic, and therefore prevent their dreams from manifesting. You, too, deserve to have your dreams come true. You deserve to live a wonderful, exciting, and rich life. Permit yourself to dream.

*To have is to Dream First.*

Most of what exists in life originated as a dream. The process of manifesting dreams begins with imagination. Dreams begin in the invisible. "I have always dreamed of having..." "I always wanted ... ""I knew someday I would...." We all have dreams. We all have desires. We wish upon stars and while blowing out birthday candles. We throw pennies into fountains. Making wishes and dreaming dreams is fun. We like to dream, and we hope that our dreams will someday come true.

Children are natural dreamers. They dream with ease and use their imaginations to the fullest. They are not intimidated by reality, and therefore immerse themselves in fantasy. Some parents go to great lengths to preserve the wonder and excitement of life for their children. They want them to hold on to the belief, the wonder, and the spirit of life for as long as possible. They want them to believe in Santa Claus, the Easter Bunny, stardust, and the man on the moon. These friends encourage childhood dreams and foster imagination and creativity.

Adults dream as well. State lotteries and scratch-off tickets offer the dream of winning and striking it rich. Adults dream about having the "good life" and basking in the land of good and plenty. They dream about owning a lovely home, driving a luxurious car, or retiring at an early age. Most adults do not admit to having dreams, as they think that dreams are silly or a waste of time. The wish list is replaced by the to-do list. Adults are practical. They learn to surrender fantasy and embrace realism. They live in the "real world," where life is serious and complex. They exchange the wonder and excitement of dreaming for the fear that their needs will not be met and the belief that they must struggle. Adults abandon the wonder and spirit of believing. They surrender the most significant tool for living a prosperous life—believing in the invisible wonder of the Universe. Instead, they work hard, struggle to achieve more, and believe that they must settle for less than what they truly desire.

There must be a better way—a simple and practical way—to accomplish your dreams and live happily ever after. If only there was a manual that told you how to make your dreams come true. You could quickly turn to a specific page and there, in print, would be instructions on how to build the life you desire. It would be easy to read and simple to apply. But even if there were such a manual, would you know what it is that you truly desire?

*What do you desire in life?*

This important life question leads you in the direction of your life. It guides you to where you are going in life. Take a moment now to answer this question. What do you desire in life? Write down your response on a piece of paper for future reference.

Although many people list monetary or material desires, a common response to this question is, "I just want to be happy."

Happiness is the most sought-after component of prosperity. People have lost sight of true happiness. Happiness has become increasingly difficult to recognize and to hold on to for an extended period. Sure, you may be able to identify specific times when you felt happy, such as on your wedding day or the day you gave birth to your child, but this implies that something must happen for you to feel happy. Happiness is not an occasion; it is a way of life.

Struggle has replaced happiness and has become synonymous with living. Most people have come to accept struggle as a necessary part of life. It is familiar. People expect things to be difficult and challenging. Struggle is a well-known factor in life. Consider for example the times that you walk through a room without turning on the light. You convince yourself that it will be quicker to walk through the unlit room than to take the time or extra steps to turn on the light. And so, you cautiously proceed through the dark, hoping and praying that you will not trip or fall. You also struggle when you carry miscellaneous data in your head—the telephone calls to make, the appointments to be scheduled, and the laundry detergent that needs to be picked up.

You prize yourself on having a good memory, while you worry about forgetting an important task or detail. Struggle is what you do when you try to save yourself a trip to the car by carrying in several bags of groceries at one time. The result, of course, is crushed bread, broken eggs, and assorted items dropped along the way. You convince yourself that your way is easier, when in fact you are struggling. You think that struggling will somehow make you stronger, but it only causes you to feel frustrated and overwhelmed. Struggle disables you. It contaminates your life. It drains your happiness and robs you of your dreams.

Struggle honors the mistaken belief that life is challenging and limited. Most people see life through the eyes of limitation. They believe that life is limited, and that all things in life are limited. They believe that there is "only so much," and unfortunately, they are the last in line to receive.

*Life is not limited.*

You create what you believe to be true. You think limitation, and therefore you live in limitation. You limit your life, your career, your finances, and yourself. You see only so much. You give only so much. You pay only so much. You do only so much. You limit yourself.

The good news is that limitation is born out of one's perceptions and not out of one's reality. That is, you think that you are limited when indeed you are never limited. Life has no limitations. Life only knows abundance. There is not merely one tree, there are many trees. There is not merely one cloud, there are many clouds. There is not merely one body of water; there are many bodies of water. You live in abundance, while thinking limitation.

The dictionary definition of prosperity reads, "The state of being prosperous; advance or gain in anything good or desirable; successful progress in any business or enterprise; success; wealth" (Webster's Unabridged Deluxe Dictionary). The term prosperous is defined as "making gain or increase; thriving; successful; well to do; well-off." The terms prosperity and abundance are often used interchangeably. In simply reviewing these definitions, one can clearly see that prosperity can consist of anything and can happen to anyone. However, prosperity is typically associated with being rich or famous.

We believe that wealth and prosperity are reserved for a select few in our society, which leaves most of us out. The truth is that you, too, are equally entitled to the prosperity and abundance that exist in this world. It resides in your own backyard as well.

Take a moment now to think about someone whom you consider to be prosperous. What is it about that person or his or her lifestyle that leads you to believe that he or she is prosperous? Is it how that person dresses or lives? Is it his or her career? What makes that person prosperous in your eyes?

Prosperity means different things to different people. Therefore, it is necessary to define prosperity in terms of your own experiences and desires. Take the time now to complete each of the following statements:

1. Prosperity, to me, is defined as . . .

2. What I desire to have in my life is . . .

3. Thus far, I am attracting to my life . . .

4. My prosperity is currently limited by . . .

5. When I am living prosperously, I . . .

From this understanding of personal prosperity, create a list of your desires currently in your life. To aid you in this process, complete the stem sentence, "I want...." Write down whatever comes to you. Do not censor or judge your response. Simply write down your dreams and desires. Once you have your list of desires, go through your list again, and number them in order of their priority to you. What is the first thing you are looking to attract into your life? In a later chapter, you will learn how to develop specific goals toward achieving your desires.

Use your list of desires as a bookmark. In this way, you will be able to revise them or check them off as you continue to work through the subsequent chapters. It also serves to keep them visible to you as you work toward achieving them. The following are the most common definitions of prosperity, which may resemble or expand on your personal definition.

MATERIAL WEALTH

Material wealth is having wonderful things in your life, such as a nice car, a beautiful home, and various toys of pleasure and leisure (boat, motorcycle, cottage on the lake). Material possessions provide a visible statement of prosperity. In fact, people make assumptions regarding people based on their material possessions. There are people who judge another person's lifestyle based on the type of car driven or the look of a home. There is the belief that if you own nice things, you "have it all."

Material wealth, or the hope of having it, is the reason people get up in the morning to go to work. You work to have wonderful things in your life. Yet prosperity includes much more than the cost or value of a person's material possessions. People will agree that material possessions alone do not make a person happy and content. Instead, a happy person is a magnet that attracts material possessions.

## FINANCIAL SECURITY/INDEPENDENCE

Financial security is a strongly desired component to prosperity. It is often associated with the belief that there is an absence of worry about money. It is the ability to have all your bills paid, money in the bank, and money in your pocket. There is freedom to buy what you want when you want it. Financial security is the knowledge and reality that the money is always there. Cash is available and "on hand." Financial security ensures a daily life of financial freedom.

Many people grew up in families where money and financial matters were not discussed, and consequently, people feel inadequate or unknowledgeable regarding financial matters. They are unaware of how to manage money and financial affairs. They feel "in the dark" regarding such a vital area of living.

The plastic society that now exists removes us from the true values of prosperity. Credit cards allow us to obtain material possessions on credit, rather than with money that is already earned. Therefore, actual money is no longer necessary to own things. Children observe that it is no longer necessary to have green paper dollars or silver coins to have things. Instead, you offer a plastic card in exchange for goods or services that you desire. The plastic card is used to get cash from machines in stores or in bank parking lots. Credit cards have led us to be a society rich in material wealth, but cash poor.

Money alone does not make a person happy or guarantee fulfillment. Financial security, like material possessions, is certainly nice to have.

However, money is only part of the equation to prosperity and living an abundant life.

## PRESTIGIOUS WORK

"So, what do you do for a living?" This is a typical question when making conversation or acquainting yourself with others. People are considered prosperous when they hold prestigious positions in large or key companies or when they have promising careers. Business owners, CEOs, and professionals, such as doctors and lawyers, are automatically put in the highest category of prosperity. It is assumed that they make good money and have all that they need.

*Work is merely the channel through which prosperity is achieved.*

Work is how you become prosperous. However, you will not achieve true prosperity by simply working; your job must also give you satisfaction. It does not matter what kind of work you do if you enjoy doing it.

## HIGHER EDUCATION

We are a society that has come to value higher education. In the past, it was not necessary (nor were you expected) to pursue a college education. Instead, you were expected to be "gainfully employed," preferably working for a big company like General Electric, IBM, or New York Telephone. Employment was the acceptable way to earn money and benefits to care for your family. Times have changed.

Societal expectations have changed regarding the need for education. We now strongly encourage our children to go to college. In fact, we expect it. We plan for it. Therefore, higher education can now be considered a component of prosperity. People assume others are prosperous based on where they attended college or how many degrees hang on their wall.

Although a higher education is valued and aids a person in obtaining prestigious work, it alone does not create a prosperous lifestyle. There are people who have numerous degrees but cannot work within their areas of education. There are also people without a college degree who live prosperously. We need to value all people in all professions. People who have chosen not to pursue a higher education are still necessary and make important contributions to our society. All types of work are needed for life to be harmonious. We cannot all be doctors and lawyers, for that would only enable us to meet our medical and legal needs. We need people in all jobs for all our needs to be met. We need the police and the firefighters, the wait-staff, and the postal employees. We need the cashiers and the flight attendants. We need the teachers and the day-care providers. Where would our lives be without all the people who hold these jobs? True prosperity does not come with a particular job title. Prosperity is enjoying the work that you do and getting paid for it.

*All professions hold the promise of prosperity.*

HEALTH

"If you have your health, you have everything." Good physical health is necessary for a prosperous and happy life. Yet, good health is often taken for granted. It is easy to overlook your ability to walk into the kitchen of your home or up a flight of stairs without physical pain or difficulty. Yet these simple and routine tasks seem almost impossible to accomplish when your health is compromised. When you are in poor health, you appreciate good health and the abilities that accompany good health. Poor health shifts your life, your affairs, and your attitude.

*Focus on good health.*

Appreciate and value your good health while you have it. Take care of yourself before you are physically ill. If you do not take care of yourself, your attitude, or your hectic work schedule, your body may do it for you. The human body can take you out of commission suddenly, and without warning. You can feel well one minute and ill the next minute. Think of your body as an alarm system that gets you to pay attention to what you are doing to yourself.

You do not have to be physically sick and in bed to give yourself permission to rest. Indulge in an occasional nap. Sit in a recliner or a hammock and read a newspaper or magazine. Take a walk in the sunshine. Relax. Replenish. Nurture and appreciate good health.

Prosperity is awareness. It is the realization that what you have is what you need. Prosperity is having an umbrella when it is raining. It is the warmth and comfort of your sheets and blankets each night. It is having gas in your car and money in your pocket when you need milk and bread.

Prosperity is recognizing that there is always plenty—plenty of resources, plenty of services, plenty of time, plenty of houses, plenty of everything you need or want.

Prosperity is simplicity. It is discovering the simple alternatives to the familiar struggle in your daily life. It is taking less, carrying less, and yet having more. It is taking the easier path through life.

Prosperity is being. It is being in the moment. It is being physically and emotionally present to what is going on in this moment rather than being distracted by what happened earlier or what will happen next.

Prosperity is enjoying life. It is playing flashlight tag with your kids on a warm summer's eve. It is singing silly songs on your way to the dry cleaners. It is being playful and spontaneous. Prosperity is having fun.

*Prosperity is the joy of living.*

In the classic story The Wizard of Oz, the Scarecrow desired knowledge, the Tin Man desired love, and the Cowardly Lion desired courage. Knowledge, love, and courage are all found within an individual. Prosperity, too, begins as a feeling within you that is then reflected on the physical world. Your thoughts and feelings possess the ability to obtain life's finest riches and to experience true prosperity. When you feel prosperous within, your external world begins to present outward signs of prosperity as well. So, like Dorothy, the key to getting what you want is always with you. Your responsibility is to first know that it is within your power, and then to act. In other words, start clicking those heels.

Cultivate the feeling of prosperity in your heart and in your mind. Prosperity brings inner peace. It is a feeling of harmony and contentment that allows a person to feel complete, satisfied, and nourished in life. There is an easier path to a happier and fulfilling life, if only you dare to try it.

*They are like trees planted by streams of water, which*
*yield their fruit in its season, and their leaves do not*
*wither. In all that they do, they prosper.*

--Psalms 1:3

In the diagram below, you can preview the Building Blocks to Manifesting your Dreams and Desires. Each concept within this pyramid will be further discussed in subsequent chapters. For now, it is only necessary for you to recognize that manifesting your desires is a process. It is a process that includes several things working consecutively to produce the desired outcome. It is a process that is enjoyable to learn, and it is extremely rewarding.

## Building Blocks to Manifesting Your Dreams and Desires

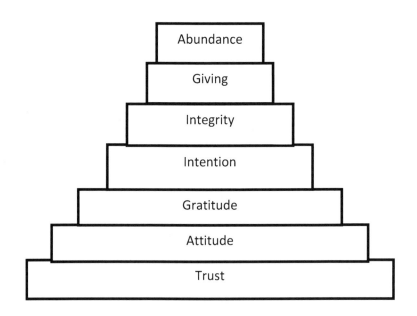

# Chapter 2

# Avoiding the Emotional Potholes to Prosperity

*Be too large for worry, too noble for anger, too strong for fear,*
*and too happy to permit the presence of trouble.*

*Optimists' Creed*

Now that you have begun the process of knowing what you want in life, it is time to take a serious look at what is blocking you from the good life. What is getting in your way and preventing you from taking the easier path through life?

There are numerous obstacles that stand in the way of being happy. Some obstacles are obvious, such as a lack of resources, opportunities, funds, or time. Most obstacles include the lack of something needed. However, the most significant obstacles to living a prosperous and fulfilling life are the various emotions that you hold regarding life, prosperity, money, and happiness.

Consider the many feelings that you have in general—anger, sadness, fear, hurt, surprise, joy, frustration, loneliness, worry, shock, confusion, and the various terms for describing each feeling. You have a feeling for everything. Therefore, your ability to manifest the good things in life is dependent on your individual emotions. There are specific feelings that usually sabotage this desired good. These powerful feelings include fear, jealousy, anger, shame, inadequacy, and discouragement.

## FEAR

Fear is the most influential emotion that sabotages prosperity. Fear paralyzes prosperity. "Fear?" you may ask. "What could I possibly be afraid of?" Most people are not aware of their fears. Fear is more apparent in the person who is afraid of heights or of flying in airplanes. People with phobias are aware of their fears and avoid such circumstances. However, there are many fears in one's life that go undetected. Take for example the common fear of not having enough money. My mother grew up in a single-parent household during the Depression. She was supported by the welfare system. She tells stories about putting cardboard in her shoes to fill the holes in them. Your parents or grandparents experienced similar hardships and financially challenging times. What you may not realize is that you may have inherited their beliefs in lack and impoverishment. Although you did not personally experience a lack of resources, money, or necessities, you may have inherited those fears from previous generations. You may have witnessed your parents experiencing financial struggle and hardship, and now fear experiencing your own financial hardship.

When you live in fear, you block your good from coming forth and manifesting in a physical way. Fear has many faces and takes many forms, yet it tends to hold the same consequences for each person. Fear impinges on life and the manifestation of dreams. Take the time to identify the fears that sabotage your dreams and goals (see appendix 1).

## Fear That Your Needs Will Not Be Met

The fear that your needs will not be met is a universal fear. This is the fear that you will be late to an event, that you will miss the bus or plane, that you will lose your job, or that your wallet will be stolen while on vacation. It is the feeling that what you need will somehow be withheld from you.

This fear tends to originate from an earlier experience in which a basic need was not sufficiently met. No matter how functional and healthy your family may have been while you were growing up, there is typically a need that did not get met or was not met sufficiently. Some people were deprived of basic needs such as food, shelter, and clothing. Abraham Maslow demonstrated in his Hierarchy of Needs that it is necessary to meet the basic physiological needs prior to meeting emotional needs (safety, security, and nurturance). That is, it would be unrealistic to alleviate symptoms of depression if someone has not eaten in two weeks.

Children are born with the basic awareness that their needs will be met. They know that what they need will be provided. It is through one's life experiences that the innate ability to trust that our needs will be met is adversely affected. Consequently, many adults do not expect that their needs will be met. Instead, their trust diminishes, and fear and worry take its place. They become anxious and dismayed. If you doubt this, just observe people in an airport. Airport travelers become frantic to get their needs met. People become anxious as they prepare to board an airplane. They rush and push their way through lines. They stand by the gate anxiously waiting for their seat number to be announced. The truth is that we live in a society that is not good at waiting. We equate waiting with the belief that our needs will not be met. While leaving a hotel for the airport, I watched a woman push her extremely large suitcase into the street to gain the attention of the oncoming shuttle bus. The shuttle bus nearly hit her baggage. She pushed her way through people to get her needs met. Her behavior communicated her strong feeling of fear that her needs would not be met. Fear does not permit a person to stand back and allow things to happen. Fear prompts action and reaction, and sometimes over-reaction.

The truth is that your needs are met when you believe that they will be sufficiently met. Yet your belief in lack is much more powerful than your belief in trust. Trust, which will be discussed in Chapter 4, is the essential ingredient needed to overcome fear.

# Fear of Being Perceived as Selfish, Greedy, or Cheap

There are people who will tell you that they do not want money or material things in their life. They are concerned that others will judge them in a negative manner. After all, the "rich are greedy," or so we have been known to think. Those who have money are "selfish" or "cheap." The truth is that there are just as many impoverished people who are selfish and greedy as there are wealthy people. Selfishness and greed are not specific attributes of only the well-to-do. The selfish or greedy person, whether rich or poor, is a very fearful person. These attributes are associated with the fear of losing what one has or of being taken advantage of by others. Fear creates a fervent desire to hold on to what you have.

There is a distinct difference between being selfish and meeting your physical and emotional needs. "Selfishness" is a judgment or negative perception of someone other than you. That is, someone else judges you to be selfish and to ignore the needs of others. Meeting one's needs requires balance and the ability to discern your needs from the needs of others.

# Fear of Not Having Enough

A common fear that blocks the flow of good is the fear of not having enough. It is the steadfast, yet often unconscious, belief that there is not enough. This fear is similar to the fear that your needs will not be met. It develops because of being denied something that was innately basic to your survival, such as love, affection, attention, food, or proper care. Thus, it is easily recreated throughout your life. It shows its ugly face in those fears about money, time, the present, and the future. It is the culprit behind bankruptcy, theft, job insecurity, and so much more. It produces the fervent desire for additional material possessions to fill the emotional void or emptiness within. There is a tendency to try to replace the internal fear of not having enough with external costly possessions. It does not work. Instead, you must let go of the fear that dwells inside. Then you can replace those familiar feelings of lack and scarcity with the belief and feeling of "good and plenty." When you feel that you are enough, you will always have enough.

## Fear of Failure

Many people struggle with the fear of failure, which is another obstacle to the receiving of good. It is the fear of not measuring up to perceived standards. It is often associated with feeling inadequate and "not good enough." Often this fear is demonstrated by lack of completion; things are left undone and incomplete. The person fears a disappointing outcome and may also be afraid of disappointing others. Therefore, the thoughts and perceptions of others weigh heavily into the fear of failure. This fear causes a person to feel afraid of making a mistake, or of not doing something right. He or she strives for perfection, and consequently often feels disappointed. Perfectionism is a form of self-sabotage.

Of course, the fear of failure can arise from a history of failed attempts or outcomes. For instance, if a man has experienced a great deal of criticism in his life, he may experience a fear of being criticized for a particular task or project. Yet, the reality is that criticism will be forthcoming for not completing the task or project. As you let go of the desire to make something perfect, you experience success in its completion.

## Fear of Success

The fear of success is the opposite of the fear of failure. The fear of success is feeling afraid of what will happen to your life once you become successful. This is the person who wants a job promotion but is afraid of how it may affect his or her life. The promotion might require travel and additional hours on the job. It is believed that it will bring dramatic and undesirable changes to your current life. There is a fear that this greater success will cost something greater.

The fear of success and the fear of failure often occur simultaneously. It is possible to be afraid of failing while also being afraid of succeeding.

It unfortunately creates a no-win situation and can lead to feeling stagnant for years.

> Jane was a talented actor who desired to be in a soap opera or a television sitcom. She loved her work. However, she would often leave successful jobs in the entertainment field and return home to her familiar rural community. While living in her community, she would care for her children and be angry with herself for not being in New York or Los Angeles pursuing her dreams. This created a double bind for her. She felt like she could not win either way. On one hand, she would pursue her dream while living without her children. On the other hand, she struggled financially and frequently resorted to working in retail just to pay her rent.

Fear creates a cycle of self-defeat. Fearful people tend to go forward and backwards to make something work. They head toward their dream, only to return to the starting line by starting over or by finding a new dream to pursue. They often struggle with depression and anxiety as they try to find the exit. The only way out is to force themselves to commit to a period of time before they "give up." In other words, they contract with themselves to be persistent and to stay on the path to success for a specific period of time. It is in doing so that they forfeit the sabotaging thoughts of failure. They need to prove to themselves that they can do it. They can succeed. Consistent therapy throughout this period is also vital, as they require the support to keep going forward. And then they do!

## Fear of Being Judged

At one time or another, we have all experienced the fear of being judged by others. How many times have you been worried about what someone else may think of you, your appearance, or your actions? We all want to be accepted and liked by others. Yet we also live in a very judgmental society. We have opinions of others—where they live, who they live with, what they do for a living, how they raise their children, what they wear, and how they live their lives. We easily put others down to feel good about ourselves. It is as if we need to condemn others before they have the chance to condemn us.

*Your judgments of others reflect*
*your personal fears and insecurities.*

We judge people as "materialistic" when we think that they own wonderful things. We too desire wonderful things, but do not believe that we have the same quality or quantity of wonderful things as others have. The simple owning of wonderful things does not make someone "materialistic." It is the attitude regarding possession than the actual possession. When others seem to idealize or worship their material possessions, we tend to judge them as "materialistic." They are also perceived as "materialistic" when they place the significance of material things over people.

The truth is that we often make judgments about others without having all the facts. We make assumptions without gaining the facts. When you judge, you are communicating that you want what others have. You are displaying your insecurities. Those who judge others are afraid of being judged. They talk and gossip about others to avoid being the target of the judgement of others. As you heal your own emotional insecurities, you are less likely to judge others. You accept others for who they are and experience the same acceptance in return.

*Stop judging and you will not be judged. Stop condemning and you will*
*not be condemned. Forgive and you will be forgiven.*

—Luke 6:37

# Fear of Being Disappointed

Life is spent trying to avoid the dreadful feeling of disappointment. Preparing for and expecting something bad to happen can elude disappointment. Consequently, most people choose to expect the worst of any situation. It seems easier to expect the worse than to expect the best. Therefore, the fear of disappointment prevents you from taking the risks necessary to pursue the life that you desire. There is no point in trying if you expect disappointment.

## Fear of Hurting Others

Most of us have a tender place in our hearts for the welfare of others. Therefore, the fear of hurting another can and often does calculate into our decisions. Sometimes, this fear leads us to sacrifice our own needs. You allow the feelings of others to affect you and to hold you back.

## Fear of Being Perceived as Poor or Impoverished

We do not want others to think badly of us in any way. We certainly do not want others to think that we lack money, resources, or basic needs. We are ashamed of what we do not have, so we go to great lengths to put forth an image, albeit a false image, to avoid being judged negatively. We do not want others to think that we "do not have." We may hold negative beliefs about those people who do not have, those who we perceive to be impoverished or poor.

## Fear of Being Perceived as Wealthy

Alas, the reverse is true as well. People feel ashamed of "having." They feel ashamed and guilty for having wonderful things. As a result, they make excuses for what they have. "Oh, my parents gave me that." "Well, it's a used car." "I have had it for a long time." It is as if we want wonderful things, but we feel embarrassed or ashamed of these wonderful things.

People can feel jealous of the material wealth of others, which can cause them to shame others for having what they do not have. Shame is distributed through common phrases such as "We're not as rich as you are," "That's right, you are the one with the education," "It must be nice to always be going on vacations," or "Oh, you can afford it." These comments are shaming and sabotage people from genuinely enjoying and appreciating the good in their lives. The judgments of others can cause you to hide your good. Hiding or minimizing your good obstructs the flow of abundance into your life. Therefore, it is important to recognize the shame that may block your manifestation of good things, as shame communicates the fact that you do not deserve such things.

Take a few minutes now to identify any shame that you feel about having money or wonderful things in your life. Close your eyes and let yourself go back to times when others shamed you for having wonderful things. Take the time to write about these experiences in a journal or notebook. The writing process will provide you with a means for identifying and releasing the shame. Complete your writing with the phrase "I now fully let go of this shame and enjoy unlimited prosperity." You get to tell yourself what you can or cannot have in your life. Do not allow the insecurities of others to determine your worth.

## Fear of Being Taken Advantage of

This fear is usually only noticed after the fact. That is, people do not feel that they have been taken advantage of until it has already happened, which causes feelings of anger and resentment. This fear develops out of previous experiences of feeling used by others and inhibits a person's willingness to share. People may hold on to things, as they fear that things will be taken from them. They may be guarded and suspicious. They do not live-in ease. Instead, they experience life as a victim in which they are vulnerable and mistrusting of others.

## Fear of Being Hurt, Harmed, or Attacked

People who are afraid of being emotionally hurt by another person tend to avoid relationships and commitments. They have had their feelings hurt and their heart broken. Since it takes a great deal of time to get over such hurt, they are reluctant to take that risk again. Some people spend years without a relationship to avoid being hurt again.

Many people have a fear of being physically harmed or attacked. It certainly has a basis in the media, where we hear horror stories day after day. Fear causes you to look over your shoulder as you walk down a dark street. Fear startles you when you hear a sudden loud noise. It is necessary to be cautious, but you do not need to be afraid. Develop the ability to trust that you are safe.

The next time someone says something to you that prompts a strong emotional reaction, seize the opportunity—close your eyes and look inward. Be willing to discover something about you. Be still and listen. Ask yourself the question, what does this situation or feeling bring up for me? What is it that I need to know? Wait and let the answer come. Be patient with yourself. As information comes forth, trace it back to another time in your life and recognize how you felt or reacted. Identify and explore the experience that left a scar. What was happening during that time in your life? What were you feeling? What were you seeing, hearing, or doing? When you have fully explored this experience, open your eyes, and write down what you have learned. Information is a source of healing.

Psychotherapists refer to this process as taking "a personal inventory." Go within and discover what is truly causing your reaction. Do not waste precious time and energy feeling defensive or blaming the other person. There may be some truth to what you are being told, even though you do not want to hear it. It may not all apply but look for what is significant and what may be helpful to know. You may be surprised to discover that the thing that bothers you about that person (his or her actions or comment) is about you. Other people are a mirror that reflects to you your own weaknesses. Therefore, you are reminded of a particular characteristic that you dislike about yourself. Perhaps it is something that you have struggled to change or to overcome for a long time. "Jill is so annoying. She is always telling people what to do." If you have heard yourself saying something similar, then there may be a part of you that tells people what to do. Or there is a part of you that would like to be able to tell someone else what to do. Of course, the list of characteristics that we find bothersome in others is often endless. Despite what we may want to believe, we are not perfect. By blaming, judging, and gossiping about others, we are often covering up our fears. These behaviors only block your desires and the fulfillment of your dreams, and life remains gray and black.

*Success and prosperity require risk.*

These are only the fears that create obstacles to having the things and experiences you want in life. Fear prevents you from taking risks. Therefore, you stay in an abusive relationship or at an unfulfilling job even though you are miserable. Many people are afraid to take the risks necessary to be happy, successful, and prosperous. They are comfortable with the familiar. They may not be satisfied, but at least they know what to expect.

Step outside of the familiar. Take the risk of being uncomfortable and scared. Risk means taking a chance for things to be better. Release the fear that disables you. Instead, embrace confidence and trust.

Although fear is the most predominate feeling that inhibits prosperity, it is certainly not the only one. It is necessary' to identify other common feelings that inhibit prosperity. These feelings include jealousy, anger, guilt, shame, inadequacy, and unworthiness. These negative feelings also pose a threat to your abundance.

JEALOUSY AND ENVY

Jealousy is nothing more than fear under an alternate disguise. It is a fear that exists in the context of human relationships. Jealousy resonates from the belief that others have it better than you do. You may think, "The grass is greener on the other side of the fence." But is it? After all, that is not your grass. You have grass, too. Why don't you feed and nourish what you have rather than envying the other side? Look at what you do have rather than what you do not have.

Jealousy arises from the fear of losing someone, the fear of being alone, or the fear of being abandoned. Some people are afraid that their significant others will cheat on them, thus they fear losing that person or relationship. Other people are emotionally, financially, or socially dependent on a spouse or partner, so they are envious when their partner spends time with friends. They feel excluded or left behind. Jealousy is accompanied by a lack of trust. Fear takes over and pushes out trust, which is a necessary component of healthy relationships. Jealousy creates possessiveness, the desire to know where someone is and what he or she is doing.

Jealousy is rooted in the past. It is only recreated in the present. Therefore, to dissolve feelings of jealousy and fear, it is necessary to trace the feelings back to their original time and experience. Hypnotherapy and EMDR (Eye Movement Desensitization and Reprocessing) are the most successful tools for accomplishing just that.

Like other fears, jealousy blocks the attraction of good in your life. For instance, if a person is jealous because of another person's college education, it not only harms the person who is jealous, but it also harms the person who "has" the education. It harms the person who is jealous in that it delays or prevents his or her own good from arriving. It harms the person who has an education because he or she feels ashamed for having the education and may be reluctant to make the most of it. This is also true regarding material wealth. To feel jealous of another person limits your ability to accept and value your personal accomplishments, and you may feel inferior and inadequate.

Refrain from envying the good that others receive, for doing so only blocks your good from coming. Instead, wish others the good that they desire. Wish them the good that you desire. If a colleague receives the promotion that you had hoped for, wish him or her well and know that your good is also on its way. Something different, something just as good or even better, is planned for you.


ANGER AND RESENTMENT

The feelings of anger and resentment also block prosperity. Anger is a normal human emotion, but it is rarely expressed in a healthy, productive manner. It is most often a cover-up for other genuine emotions, such as hurt or shame. Anger keeps people at a distance and often destroys relationships.

Resentment is holding on to negative feelings or negative events long after the actual experience. Resentment is often the culprit behind holding grudges and using the "silent treatment." Anger and resentment block the flow of good, so it is important to talk kindly to others and about others. Your good depends on it. Do not bring up issues and things of the past. Discuss matters of today, not yesterday. Develop the ability to let go and to forgive so you can move beyond negative feelings and experiences.


## SHAME AND UNWORTHINESS


Shame is a difficult feeling to address, as it is the most concealed emotion. It is the feeling that carries the most weight as it conveys a feeling of being inherently "bad" and undeserving of good. Although shame is not an obvious feeling, it exists in each person to some degree.

Parents, siblings, teachers, and bosses might have shamed you without you even realizing it. You are sometimes shamed for who you are, what you feel, what you know or do not know, and what you have or do not have. Shame carries with it the common feeling of not being "good enough." It is a feeling of inadequacy and inferiority and is typically accompanied by unworthiness or "not deserving." Shame convinces you that you do not have the right to have good things in your life. It prevents you from asking for more money or seeking a better job. It tells you to take what you can get.

Unworthiness is feeling defeated before being defeated. Unworthiness develops from life experiences in which you did not feel valued or important. Shame and unworthiness are emotional roadblocks to your desired good. They inhibit you from pursuing your dreams and desires. If you believe that you are not worthy of having good things in life, you stagnate in that belief. You are paralyzed from moving forward in your life.

Shame is often accompanied by blame. "See what you did? You are so stupid." "I can't believe you. What were you thinking?" "Are you really that stupid?" "What's wrong with you?" "You are just like your (father, mother)." "Why can't you be more like your (sister, brother)?" Shame also takes the form of name calling.

Shame is simply another way of judging other people, but with heavier weights. When a person is angry, he or she may use shame as ammunition. Shame is like giving someone a lit stick of dynamite. Emotional death can occur. Although shame is a heavy burden to carry, it is too easily dispensed. Avoid shaming others simply because you are upset or angry. Your feelings will pass, but shame leaves permanent scars.


INADEQUACY


Inadequacy is the feeling of "not being good enough." It is a feeling that prevents you from feeling confident in what you do. Men are prone to feeling inadequate. Perhaps it is related to the emphasis that is placed on the performance of men in this society. Society expects remarkable things from men. This, of course, does not mean that women are exempted from feeling inadequate. The lives of women tend to be family-focused, while the lives of men tend to be career-focused. Most people look for recognition for the good that they do, for their abilities and accomplishments. However, when you are told that you cannot do something or that you do not do something right, you are left with feeling inadequate.

DISCOURAGEMENT


Discouragement is a common feeling that suppresses prosperity. It is easy to feel discouraged. Take for example the common and mundane task of paying monthly bills. This recurrent task can take a household down in only minutes. One person questions where the money has gone, while the other one feels blamed and accused. The task of paying bills becomes a tug of war, which only magnifies the apparent lack of money. Discouragement can lead to blame. Blame only distances people from one another, and rarely provides a solution.

Discouragement also comes when you feel impatient because the thing you desire has yet to come to fruition. You become doubtful and fearful, which only further delays your desired good.

Do not discourage. Do not despair. Trade in the feelings of fear, doubt, and discouragement for the feeling of trust (described in chapter 4). For now, try on the feeling that all is okay. "Don't worry; it will be "okay." That is all you need to know to keep going. It will be okay. Your good will find its way to you.

*It will be okay.*

Eliminate all feelings of lack. There is no lack. There is only abundance. Be persistent. Prosperity loves persistence. It is so unfortunate how often we get within inches of the finish line but do not cross it. Instead, we reach exhaustion and give in to discouragement. What we really need is a final burst of energy and enthusiasm to push past the finish line. When feeling discouraged, it is time to push harder. You are almost where you desire to be.

Take a few minutes now to write down your own feelings about prosperity, both past and present. Be as specific as possible so you can understand your feelings because your feelings can get in the way of your success. Leave space for expanding your thoughts and feelings as you work your way through the subsequent chapters. Life is merely a learning curve.

Invite good feelings into your daily routine and protect them from the negative feelings of others. Do not let anyone or anything contaminate your good feelings. Life is rich with the good feelings of joy, love, peace, and happiness.

# Chapter 3

## "A Penny for Your Thoughts"

*If we look at the path, we do not see the sky; we are earth people on a spiritual journey to the stars. Our quest, our earth walk is to look within, to know who we are, to see that we are connected to all things, that there is no separation, only in the mind.*

*—Native American, Source Unknown*

Your thoughts influence your life. Unfortunately, it is the negative thoughts that seem to flow with ease, sometimes without conscious awareness. Take for example a simple conversation between two people:

Person 1: "How are you?"

Person 2: "Oh, could be better. How are you?"

Person 1: "Busy. All I do is work. They are talking about a job layoff. I'm guessing I will be out of work by Christmas."

Person 2: "Oh, really. I know what that is like. It is not like you can even prepare yourself. You cannot even save for it, at least we couldn't. Money is always so tight. You just work to pay your bills. There is never anything left over."

Person 1: "Exactly. I do not even know if it is worth it. Sometimes I think I should just quit my job and apply for welfare. I could just sit home and still be in the same position."

Negative thoughts consume your daily life and affairs. Common dialogue reflects this negative thinking. You think failure before you think success. You think defeat before you think victory. Therefore, it may not be surprising that your prosperity is blocked.

Negative thoughts are obstacles to achieving success and prosperity. Your thoughts affect your experiences. The mind is that powerful. Negative thoughts sabotage the attraction of good into your life.

*Thoughts, whether spoken or unspoken, are the means*
*with which we succeed or fail.*

Your thoughts influence your feelings and perceptions about life. Consider for a moment just the many negative thoughts and euphemisms about money that you may have learned along life's journey:

- Money does not grow on trees

- Hard-earned money

- The rich get richer, the poor get poorer

- The love of money is the root of all evil

- Time is money

- Another day, another dollar

- You either have time or money; not both

- It is the price you must pay

- Nothing is free

- Rendered penniless

Phrases such as these shape and color our thoughts, and these thoughts affect our relationship with money. Again, the negativity that exists in our everyday language becomes noticeable. In this case the negativity is about money and financial matters. These phrases lead a person to perceive money as "bad," and instill a belief that money is evil and not worth having.

Money is often a source of conflict between people. People argue over money. Take for example, the degree to which some people will go to gain inheritance money. Money has been known to alienate people and has torn families apart. People will use you if you happen to have money. You are greedy if you are not generous with others. These negative beliefs instill a feeling of discomfort and unease regarding financial matters. Some people would prefer to be without money to avoid dealing with the problem's money can create. Thus, money can "burn a hole in your pocket." You lose it. You spend it carelessly. You give it away. You deny having it. You feel guilty and ashamed for having money, and therefore you do not keep that "evil stuff' around.

It is important to examine your personal beliefs about money and other forms of prosperity. It may be helpful to begin with identifying your earliest experiences with money Can you recall your very first experience with it? Did you get an allowance? Did you have a paper route? Did you witness your parents arguing over money? What did you learn from these experiences? Did you learn that money was bad or not worth having? It is those early experiences that flavor your current relationship with money.

You may also want to examine your experiences regarding time and material possessions. Were you often told to "hurry up" as a child? Were you teased for having or not having nice clothes? Identify those beliefs that continue to impinge upon your life of prosperity.

Negative thoughts impede the attraction of good into your life. Therefore, you may find it helpful to write down your thoughts and negative beliefs that block your prosperity. See the Attitude Assessment included in the appendix.

You may also want to keep a journal of your thoughts as you work your way through this book. It will help you to identify destructive thoughts and then transfer them from your mind on to paper. Negative thoughts cannot hurt paper in the way that they can adversely affect your mind. Write down your current thoughts about prosperity, money, and material possessions. Writing down your thoughts is an appropriate means for expression. It also fosters greater clarity. And, most importantly, it frees up your mind for more important matters.

Start a "thoughts notebook." A thoughts notebook differs from a journal in that it holds ideas and thoughts, as well as the daily tasks that you are trying to remember to do. Avoid cluttering your mind with the frivolous details of your daily life. Pick up mail, drop off dry cleaning, call the utility company, purchase garbage bags, and pick up bread—it is not necessary to carry all that information around in your head. A thoughts notebook makes life easier. You will accomplish more in a shorter period, as it will keep you focused and on task. You will worry less. If things are written down, you are less likely to forget them. A small notebook makes a perfect thoughts notebook. It is easy to carry and keeps all pertinent information in one place. The thoughts notebook will save you a great deal of time and emotional energy. Your time and energy are best used elsewhere.

*Negative beliefs imply lack and limitation.*

Negative beliefs reflect the fear that your needs will not be met. It is as if you are programmed to think that whatever you need will not arrive on time or go as planned. The bus will be late. The car will not start. The tax refund check will not come. Sadly, you think such things with great certainty. Yet these thoughts are quite contradictory to what you genuinely want to have happen. You really want the bus to be on time and the check to arrive.

A gentleman seated on a plane appears anxious when his scheduled flight is delayed due to ice. He conveys to the attendant that he only has twenty minutes between the arrival of this flight and his connecting flight. He is consumed by his fear of missing his next flight. He tells the attendant, "I am not going to have enough time!"

He continues to squirm nervously in his chair as his eyes fixate on his watch.

These are the familiar thoughts of "There's not enough time; I'll never make it." These thoughts are then typically followed up with "I knew it; It happens all the time." It is second nature to think "the bad" before you think "the good." You are more likely to think that things will not work out, than you are to think that they could work out.

> Michelle and Bob had just been married. They had planned a Caribbean cruise for their honeymoon. Although they were excited for the trip, they repeatedly told others of the catastrophes they had experienced on previous trips. "Things always go wrong when we take a vacation." Upon their return from the honeymoon, they reported on the experience. "The weather was lousy. We were both seasick most of the time. The food was more than we could eat." In addition, they had overslept one day, and therefore missed a planned excursion. They were unable to get their money refunded due to their own error. Their honeymoon had just been another disappointing trip.

Without realizing it, Michelle and Bob had created their experience through their thoughts prior to having the actual experience. This is commonly referred to as "anticipating the bad." Negative thoughts taint your experiences.

*Your chosen beliefs affect your actual experiences.*

Your thoughts initially convey your desires. That is, your thoughts inadvertently speak of what you wish to have happen and begin the process of making your dreams a reality. Therefore, your thoughts must coincide with your visions and your dreams. Use the power of your mind to your benefit, rather than for your destruction. Learn to think the best of a situation or circumstance, regardless of your fears. Your specific thoughts can and often do manifest into reality.

*Positive thoughts = Positive life experiences*
*Negative thoughts = Negative life experiences*

Positive thoughts aid you in creating positive life experiences. They provide you with the necessary ingredients for making something good happen. Positive thinking is one component of prosperity that is within your reach. You can think positively. You can choose to think in terms of your desires rather than in terms of your fears. It is possible to think "plenty" rather than "not enough." It is possible to think "abundance" instead of "lack." Recall a time when you were expected to be somewhere at a specific time. Review your thoughts throughout the process. Were you thinking lack or abundance?

You start with jumping in your car and speeding down the road to make up for "lost time." Then you innocently glance down at the clock and think, Oh no! I am not going to make it. I am going to be late. This is a daily experience for some of us, is it not? We do it all the time. We race to the post office thinking that if we do not hurry, it will be closed when we get there. We make ourselves frantic. Fears make us frantic. When you think that things will not work out in the way that you had hoped, you are creating what is commonly referred to as a "self-fulfilling prophecy." It is the belief that what you profess to be true comes true. And so, when you believe that you will not be on time, you will not be.

Doesn't it make more sense to believe what you want to have happen in your life rather than to believe what you do not want to have happen? It takes the same amount of energy to think abundance as it does to think lack. However, there is less anxiety when you can tell yourself, "I will be on time, and it will be okay." Experience the difference that positive thinking makes in your life. It is truly a benefit to think in a positive and productive manner.

*Embrace thoughts that will enrich your life.*

Develop a prosperity consciousness that is conducive to what you want to experience. Acquire a mindset in which you believe that only good things happen. Believe the good in all situations and circumstances regardless of what "reality" presents.

> While traveling on a business trip, Irene needed three stamps to mail bills that were due. It was a Sunday morning when she realized that she had not yet mailed the bills. She immediately focused her thoughts on locating three stamps and mailing the bills. She went to the hotel desk and was informed that they were out of stamps. She did not give up. She decided to get a cab to take her to the post office. Although she did not think the post office would be open on a Sunday, she thought there might be a machine that sold stamps. Upon arriving, she discovered that this post office was open seven days a week, twenty-four hours a day. She bought the stamps and handed her mail to the clerk behind the counter.

Prosperity demands that you believe that all things are possible. If Irene had chosen to believe that post offices are closed on Sundays, she would not have made the attempt to go to the post office. She would have surrendered to negative thoughts. Prosperity consciousness is the knowledge that you will have whatever you need. Thinking in such a way produces the most rewarding and often surprising life experiences.

> *Prosperity is not what you have or how much you make.*
> *It is how you think.*

Be mindful of your thoughts. It is too easy to slide into impoverished thinking and the familiar feelings of lack and limitation. Keep a positive attitude. When in doubt, believe that things are working out. Choose to believe that your needs will be met.

> While on a Caribbean vacation, Robin discovered that thirty dollars was missing from her hotel room. She

believed that the housekeeping staff had taken her money. She quickly warned her friends not to leave money visible in their rooms. A friend told Robin, "Maybe the housekeeper thought it was her tip." Robin angrily replied, "Well, I'm not giving her any more money then."

This serves as a common example of a person's tendency to think impoverishment. Robin's immediate thoughts were that of theft and of being taken advantage of. How often have you jumped to a conclusion such as this and later discovered that you had misplaced your money? This is evidence of how easy it is to paint a picture of lack and limitation rather than abundance.

I once had a similar experience while vacationing in Atlantic City. Without realizing it, I had left money on the kitchen counter of a hotel suite. When the money was missing (notice the word missing instead of taken), I realized that the housekeeper might have perceived it as her tip. However, rather than warn my friends that there may be thieves among us, I chose to let it go and not react in fear or dismay. I believed that there must have been a reason for this experience to happen. I do not usually leave money sitting on a kitchen counter of a hotel. It was certainly an oversight on my part. Rather than begrudge another person, I affirmed that the money went into the right hands and that I, too, would have my financial needs met. The next day, I won enough money at the casino to cover the tip as well as my expenses for the week of the vacation.

Adopt a prosperous attitude. Think the good before you think the bad. Encourage others to think in terms of abundance rather than lack. Positive thoughts fuel the energy that attracts the good into your life. They clear the path to make your dreams come true.

Unfortunately, money is a common ground for conflict and tense arguments. Some people would rather pay the entire bill at a restaurant than negotiate who owes what. The bill is promptly paid to avoid the discomfort associated with asking for or receiving money from others.

Financial matters are often at the heart of conflict in marriages today. Conflict stems from feelings of fear, doubt, or uncertainty.

Disagreements occur regarding how money is saved, as well as how money is spent. Unless a couple has unlimited amounts of money and similar perceptions about money, they will experience disagreement and conflict. Many people are fearful of spending money, as they are afraid that the money will not be there for the necessary things in life, such as their mortgage payment.

Conflict repels money. Therefore, if you and your spouse fight over money, you are obstructing the flow of money to you. Your money will easily go out but will not always find its way back to you. Prosperity is attracted to harmony, and it is harmony that produces further prosperity.

People grow up with various beliefs and experiences regarding money, and because of this, couples tend to have differing views and approaches when it comes to dealing with money. Some people adopt beliefs that are like their parent's beliefs, while others attempt to disengage from the negative beliefs of their parents.

It is rare to have two people in a relationship who are both conservative savers. A relationship is more likely to consist of one who saves and one who spends. The saver is typically afraid of not having enough money, while the spender feels denied of material things. Savers are selective in their spending. They typically live below their means so they can save and invest their money. They often choose to "go without." Although this is quite effective in achieving financial success, the attitude of the saver is usually one of scarcity and lack. They have money, but they do not believe that they have money. Savers can react defensively when others ask them for money. They resist giving their money for fear of not having enough. They are not willing to give or to spend their "hard-earned" money.

> John and his wife Karen have been married for fourteen years. John is a saver. Karen is a spender. Their differences regarding money cause a great deal of conflict in their relationship. John becomes angry any time Karen makes a purchase, even if it is something that she justifies as needing for the household. To avoid John's anger, Karen hides her purchases and receipts.

John accuses Karen of spending money foolishly. Karen feels John is "stingy" and hoards the money.

People tend to be secretive regarding their financial affairs. They do not want others to know how much money they have, how much money they earn, or how much money they spend. There is a great deal of shame surrounding money. Yet money is only money. When you project your negative thoughts and feelings onto money you give it too much power over your life.

Money has been given too much power. Everyone is in pursuit of more of it, often at the expense of enjoying life. We sacrifice time for our families and ourselves. We rob ourselves of having fun while still complaining that we do not have enough money.

Adopt an attitude about money that adds color and vibrancy to your life. Money is nice, but it is not everything. Money is a means with which you meet your needs. Money is not the actual need.

My mother has been an inspiration to me regarding my perception of money and prosperity. She could make a five-dollar bill last an entire week because of her exceptional attitude toward money. She begins with honoring the belief that five dollars is plenty of money for what she needs. She is great at anticipating what to expect and what may be needed. She always has what she needs. For example, she can take her grandchildren to the park for an entire day with sandwiches, juice boxes, and various snacks. She may then buy an ice cream for each child while at the park. The children feel like they had a million-dollar day for less than five dollars. On the other hand, there are people who would not take the time to pack such items, which will undoubtedly be wanted by children at the park, so they spend a great deal more money. Consequently, a fifty-dollar bill does not seem to be enough.

You have a relationship with money in the same way that you have relationships with people. What is your relationship with money? Do you have a love-hate relationship with it? You hate to talk about money. Money makes you feel uncomfortable. You desire it, but it is also a source of stress and discomfort.

Perhaps you have a detached relationship with money. You tend to ignore your money until you absolutely must deal with it. You dislike, and often avoid, balancing your checkbook. You have trouble keeping track of your money. You are unaware of how much money is in your bank account, in your pocket, or lying on your dresser. It is not that you do not care about your money; you just do not want to keep track of it.

On the other hand, if you have an obsessive relationship with money, you are likely to be very attentive to your financial matters. You check and recheck your balances for accuracy. You add and subtract easily in your head. You calculate everything to the penny. You always know how much money you have and how much you need.

Similarly, if you have a controlling relationship with money, you pay close attention to your finances. You carefully monitor your income and expenses. Your decisions are based on how much money you have or do not have. Money controls your decisions.

*Create harmony in your relationship with money,*
*just as in your interpersonal relationships.*

Develop a healthy relationship with money, a relationship in which you appreciate it without worshipping it. You give money as easily as you receive it. Fear no longer controls your wallet and your bank account. Instead, you make conscious choices about spending and saving. You buy what you need and only what you love.

Take the time to write a letter to money, as described in the exercise that follows. It will offer you insight into your own relationship with money.

A LETTER TO MONEY

Take out a sheet of paper. Write a letter to money in the same way that you might write a letter to an old friend whom you have not seen in a while. The following is an example.

Dear Money:

Where have you been hiding? I have been looking for you in so many places, and yet cannot seem to find you. It is as if I misplaced you. Where did you go? I need you. Life is a struggle without you. Please make your presence known so that I may feel more at ease. I know that I have been careless in taking care of you. I just push you away as if I do not need you. But I do. I do need you. I know that I need to feel more comfortable with you. I need to respect you and pay attention to you. Perhaps then I will not keep misplacing you.

Sincerely,

Fran

A prosperous and joyful life is dependent upon a positive attitude. It is not how much you do or do not have, but how you think about money and other means of prosperity. It is necessary to hold favorable thoughts about all matters in your life.

Money is only one way in which we experience the fear of not having enough. There are other areas of life that can be contaminated by such a fear. For example, there are people who spend an exorbitant amount of money on groceries. They believe that food is necessary, and therefore accept that whatever it costs, it costs. Many people need to have the cupboards full, even overflowing. Yet they may look in them and perceive them to be bare. "There is nothing to eat." Perception can differ from reality. It is not an issue of not having food, but an issue of the current selection. What they are saying is, "I don't like what is in here."

When you think that the cupboards are bare, you tend to buy more food and are likely to return to the grocery store even sooner. While grocery shopping, how many times have you thought, I better get it now, so that I do not have to come back? Or I better get that now since it is on sale? Warning: Watch out for the "Get It Now" syndrome. This syndrome is impoverished thinking. It implies that you will not have the time to get it later. It convinces you that you will not have thirty cents more when the item is no longer on sale. Impoverished thinking leads you back into the same store two days later to pick up something that you forgot to get, and to purchase more things that you think you may want later. You are fearful of being without. Therefore, you attempt to get all that you think you will need. This leads to having more of the things you already have and less of what you need. Now you not only fill your cupboards, but you must build a pantry to hold all the extras.

Some people have their own grocery stores in their basements. They possess the philosophy of "Just in case." In case of what? Are they afraid that there will be a power outage and the electronic doors to the local grocery store will not let them in? Of course not. They "stock up" because they are afraid of being without. Keeping food in storage alleviates fear. They convince themselves that it is good to have extra "because you just never know what could happen."

*We have more of the things we already have and*
*less of what we need.*

Food, to some people, is like clothing to others. Some people like their closets full and flowing with abundance. Yet they look at their wardrobe and still think that they have nothing to wear. The perception is one of "lack" rather than "abundance." It is the thought that no matter how much you have of something, it is "not enough." People tend to accumulate so many material possessions, only to think that they do not have enough. They may have too much. Our culture has too much of the things we do not want and not enough of the things we do want. Shift your thinking to abundance. Know that you will always have what you need. If you do not have something yet, believe that it will manifest when the time is right. Eliminate thoughts of lack and limitation and replace these defeating thoughts with thoughts of abundance and prosperity. Develop a belief that what you have at this moment, at any given moment, is plenty.

*Whatever you have is plenty.*

Airlines began to charge for suitcases when suitcases became so large and heavy. Prior to the weight limit, people were hauling suitcases that are as big as the human body. This behavior only exemplifies how people think that they need extraordinary amounts of things to feel satisfied. It is difficult to believe that there is always enough to meet your needs. Fear causes you to overcompensate. That is, you make sure that you have more than enough. To have enough of something no longer feels satisfying. You need more. You ask for more, you look for more, you pack more, and you borrow more. Consequently, you worry more.

Worry is fear expressed in an acceptable form. We can be worried, but rarely admit to feeling afraid. As a child, my mother often said that 99 percent of what people worry about never happens. The sad truth is that people waste precious time and energy on worrying. For example, consider how we reacted when faced with the uncertainty about the new millennium. It created a Y2K madness, and many people were terrified that their needs would not be met on January 1, 2000.

They became preoccupied, personally, and professionally, with preparing for the "what ifs." It gave everyone the chance to exercise their existing fears that their needs would not be met. They bought generators and flashlights. They stocked up on bottled water and canned food. The entire year of 1999 was spent preparing for a disaster that thankfully never happened. If anything, this experience demonstrates how we create more stress in our lives when we are afraid that our needs will not be met.

Time is also a source of stress in our lives. What are your common thoughts about time? Do you feel that you usually have enough time? Or do you feel like you run out of time? Time, like money, can inappropriately control your life. We perceive time as limited, and so that is what it becomes—limited. Yet the number of minutes and hours in a day do not change. The number of days in a year does not typically change, except for leap years. We all look forward to the extra day or the extra hour for daylight saving time. We are extremely conscious of time. Our lives are too often dictated by it and some people feel lost if they are without their watch or telephone for even a brief period.

The reality is that most people do not know how to use time to their advantage. We do not know how to appreciate time. We are too busy rushing around like we are going to miss something. And that something could be absolutely anything--an event, an activity, an airplane, a phone call. Whatever it is, we think we will miss it, and this translates to the familiar belief that our needs will not be met. No matter how much time we have, we are wizards at convincing ourselves that it will not be enough. Time, like money, has a great deal of power over our daily lives. Everyone needs to know when to start, when to end, and when to go, all of which are determined by that thing on the wall or on our wrist. Most of the world's anxiety is related to feeling that there is not enough time.

How often have you heard someone say, "If only there were more hours in a day . . ."? But it is not necessary to create more time. The Universe has been gracious enough to provide all of us with exactly the right amount of time we need. However, it is our thoughts of lack that sabotage us from experiencing time as abundant. Just the thought that there is not enough time eats away at our time. You are less efficient when you live in fear and lack.

*"I have plenty of time."*

The next time you feel anxious about not having enough time, affirm instead, "I have plenty of time." It seems hard to imagine that such an affirmation could produce more time, but it does. The truth is that when you are anxious, upset, or fearful, you are more prone to making mistakes. This, of course, costs you more time. It causes you to run back into the house for things you forgot. It requires you to redo things, which takes more time. The next time you are feeling fearful of not having enough time, shift your thinking to the idea of plenty and abundance. Repeat again and again, "There is plenty of time, all is well . . . my needs are always met." Just see what happens.

Believe it or not, simply believing that you have enough time is so much more enjoyable. The ability to trust that all your needs will be met allows you to let go of the outcome and trust that your Higher Power will see to it that everything goes as is divinely planned. You will quickly discover that you have more time to enjoy life, more time to "smell the roses." Instead of frantically running around, you will take the time to walk a beach, drink a cup of cappuccino, and still get to where you need to go. You will also be much more enjoyable to be around. Your attitude is contagious and affects those around you.

*Think only wellness.*

Since good health is a necessary component to enjoying the good life, pay attention to your thoughts about your health and wellness. Maintain positive thoughts about your health. Even when you have a cold, affirm that all is well. Negative thinking gives birth to physical symptoms of illness. Louise Hay, author of Heal Your Body, speaks of the emotional connections to physical health. Her book provides valuable insight into how fear and other feelings affect one's health. Of course, that does not mean that thinking positively will immune you from any illness or disease. Sometimes you get ill no matter how you live or how you think. However, positive thoughts have been known to add years to a person's life.

Avoid thinking the worst, as you may have been doing for so long. Think only the best. If you want something good to happen, think only good. The medical test will be negative, the appointment will be available, the doctor will be on time, and all is well.

Positive thinking is a technique that has been around for ages. Do you remember the sweet little girl in the movie Miracle on 34th Street? She desperately wanted a home with a backyard and a swing. Despite feeling discouraged, she repeatedly affirmed in the back seat of the car, "I believe, I believe, I believe." Choose to believe.

*When you believe, anything is possible.*

Train yourself to think of things going well, working out, and happening in only the best or perfect way. Put on a new pair of glasses so you can view your life differently. Become prosperous in your thinking and in your actions. Look at prosperity as the artist's palette of bright and bold colors. You are the artist, and your life is the canvas on which you paint and create your desires in life. So, begin your own journey of prosperity right now. In the wise words of Tinkerbell, "Clap three times if you believe . . ."

# Chapter 4

# Faith: Developing the Ability to Trust

When you come to the edge of all the light you know and are about to step off into the darkness of the unknown, Faith is knowing one of two things will happen: There will be something solid to stand on or you will be taught how to fly.

--Barbara J. Winter

Trust is the foundation on which you build your dreams and manifest your desires. Trust is defined in the dictionary as "confidence; a reliance or resting of the mind on integrity, veracity, justice, friendship, or other sound principle of another person or thing" (Webster's Deluxe Unabridged Dictionary). Although the concept of trust is quite simple, it is rarely maintained for more than a brief period.

Most people seek to have more of what they currently do not have—more material possessions, more money, more time. It does not matter what they want, they just want to have more of it. And when they feel the need to have more, they are working from a place of fear rather than trust. Trust is the opposite of fear. Yet fear is the familiar response to situations and circumstances. Imagine yourself on a trapeze swing, forty feet from the ground. Your hands clutch the bar for dear life. You are paralyzed with fear. Your safety depends on the successful "catch" of another trapeze artist. You are suddenly aware that the only way down is to let go. You are called to take a risk and to trust in the ability of yourself and the other person. As your hands tire, you convince yourself that you must try or simply fall to the ground. You release the bar and trust.

Fear will rarely get you to where you need to go. Instead, you feel powerless and immobilized, uncertain of what to do. Fear prevents you from moving forward. It keeps you where you are and keeps the things in your life as they are. Fear fosters stagnation.

We most often experience fear when it comes to our needs. We are afraid that our needs will not be met. We believe that the check is delayed, the doctor is unavailable, and that it will rain on the day of the outdoor wedding. Whatever we need is quickly sabotaged by whatever we fear. We react with fear rather than trust.

*Trust that your needs are always met.*

Fear makes you anxious, and therefore prompts you to control experiences and outcomes. Fear wants to know what is to be expected and what is going to happen next. Fear causes you to react, while trust allows you to observe. Fear invites negative experiences while trust invites positive experiences. Fear moves you back in life while trust moves you forward. Laurie had finally made it to the Bahamas for her Club Med vacation. She was struggling to pull a large suitcase up a flight of stairs. An onlooker offered assistance and said, "Why didn't you let the staff take your luggage to your room?" Laurie responded, "Oh, I thought it would be easier to do it myself."

How often have you convinced yourself that doing it yourself was easier than asking someone to help? Although this can look like the need to be self-sufficient, it is many times the fear that your needs will not be sufficiently met. It seems easier to rely on yourself than to risk disappointment or rejection.

*Trust minimizes the struggle.*

There are various kinds of trust. Trust takes the form of trusting yourself, trusting others, trusting outcomes or circumstances, and trusting God. Sometimes there is greater trust in one area than in another.

How well do you trust yourself? You trust yourself enough to know that you will not rob a bank this week. Your values would not allow you to give in to your fears to that degree. But how well do you trust yourself when it comes to your daily life and experiences? Do you trust your decisions? Do you trust your judgment of things? Do you value your opinions?

Trust in yourself means that you trust what you say, what you think, and what you do. Problems arise because self-doubt is known to be stronger than self-trust. Doubt looks for others to validate your personal feelings and opinions. Therefore, you ask other people what they think rather than trusting your own thoughts.

Trusting yourself includes the ability to accept yourself. It is the acceptance of your own opinions and decisions. There is no need to look elsewhere because your answers come from within. You trust your "gut feeling" or intuition without question. The opinions of other people are simply that—other peoples' opinions. Trust means that you value yourself. It is the knowledge that what you think and what you feel matters.

Trust allows you to listen to your inner wisdom or divine wisdom. Ask yourself the question, "What is my gut feeling (inner wisdom) telling me?" Honor yourself by honoring your inner wisdom. Develop trust in yourself.

Trust also comes in the form of trusting other people, a trust that is frequently challenged. People who were abused or neglected find it difficult to trust that others will not harm them. Past experiences lead them to associate trust with abuse. Therefore, they do not trust others as a means of survival. We live in a society in which trusting others can be detrimental. Trust has been replaced by the strong need for caution.

Trust is most frequently compromised when promises are broken. Although broken promises usually occur without much thought or consideration, they associate trust with disappointment.

Although it can take years to build trust, it can take an instant to evaporate. If you have been hurt or disappointed in the past, you tend to expect hurt or disappointment in the present. It is not that you want to experience disappointment; it is simply the belief that "history repeats itself."

> Mary is a retired widow who has had numerous life experiences in which men have either taken advantage of her or have not been there for her in times of need. She was interested in renovating her home; however, when her male contractor would not return her telephone calls, she assumed that the job would not get done. Based on previous negative experiences, she did not trust that her needs would be met. When the contractors completed the job, she was still dissatisfied.

Mary had developed an emotional filter through which she perceived men as manipulators. As a result of past experiences, she had lost her trust in men. As her expectations of the contractor were challenged, she adopted her previous beliefs about men. "Men cannot be trusted. Men take advantage of me. Men will deceive women." These are emotional decisions that occur at a subconscious level. They cause emotional patterns to repeat. Thus, we find ourselves in similar circumstances or reacting to situations just as we did in the past. Children of divorce are at risk for divorce. Children of alcoholics are at risk for alcoholism.

However, history does not have to repeat itself. Emotional and behavioral patterns develop out of fear. These patterns can be interrupted with the right kind of help. Surrender the fear and embrace trust. Around every corner is the opportunity to either fear or to trust. The choice is yours.

Trust takes practice. Each time that you choose trust, it is easier than the time before. Trust takes time and energy. It requires you to pay attention. Fear, not trust, is the automatic response. Trust and fear cannot exist simultaneously. You either have trust or you have fear. Trust must replace fear.

For some people, it is easier to trust a situation than it is to trust a person. How well do you trust various situations, circumstances, and outcomes? This is where control tries to wedge its way into your life. Trusting situations and outcomes is challenging. It requires you to trust that whatever happens is what is supposed to happen. You exchange your fear and worry for trust. You trust that the weather will be wonderful, your children will be safe, the train will arrive on time, and the surgery will go well. You put your trust in the situation and see what happens.

Trust is also known for its association with spiritual beliefs and practices. Trust is having faith in a spiritual presence greater than the self— the Universe, God, or Higher Power. There are many names for the many spiritual teachers, such as God, Creator, Jesus, Mother Mary, Goddess, Angels, Buddha, Jehovah, Holy Spirit, or Divine Presence. Trust is the recognition that a spiritual presence or being prevails over your life. Trust is the belief that you are safe.

Faith and trust are two words that are typically used interchangeably. Faith incorporates trust. Faith asks you to trust in someone or something that is not visible to the human eye. Therefore, faith poses a challenge to many people. They "have to see it to believe it." Instead of trust, they want proof that something exists. It is difficult to believe in, much less trust, something they cannot see. First you believe and then you trust. This is the premise from which spirituality develops.

To trust is to do so without unmistakable evidence. It believes without seeing. Take, for example, the air you breathe each moment of every day. Your breath is easily ignored and rarely visible (except in the winter months, of course), therefore you are not consciously aware of your breath unless you are experiencing a problem with breathing. Yet your life depends on your breath. The breath, although invisible, is vital to the life of the body. How can something invisible be so vital to life? And so, it is like faith. Faith is vital to your life, although not visible. Faith requires you to trust in the invisible as well as in the visible. You trust that things will work out, even when it does not appear that things will work out. You trust that you will be admitted to the graduate program prior to the acceptance letter. You trust before you see the physical evidence.

*In his hand is the life of every living thing*
*and the breath of every human being.*

--Job 12:10

Trust begins with developing a belief in a spiritual presence or being, also referred to as a spiritual connection. Although many people were raised from childhood with spiritual beliefs and practices, there are other people who feel lost regarding spirituality. Perhaps they were not exposed to spiritual beliefs, they lost sight of their previous beliefs, or they simply disagreed with what they had been taught. Spirituality grows in the same way that a person grows and matures. Some people start their spiritual journey at an early age while others begin the process sometime later in life.

If you do not currently have a spiritual connection, I encourage you to discover your own spiritual truth. Spirituality lives within an individual and can therefore be customized by your own beliefs and experiences. It is not necessary to subscribe to someone else's beliefs unless, of course, those beliefs fit with your own. For many people, the path of spirituality begins outside of the self (the external) and then gradually moves toward an internal perspective.

Spirituality includes the belief that your spiritual connection created you and provides you with all things necessary for life. Yet rarely does the typical person utilize the powerful resource of spirituality. How many times a day do you think about where you are, how you got there, and how things evolve around you and for you? How often do you look beyond what you see?

I grew up in an Irish Catholic family. My family went to church every Sunday. We prayed familiar prayers repeatedly and sometimes without real awareness of the meaning of the words recited. That, of course, is a part of the external process and the structure, which is provided so that a community of believers can worship together. However, with prayer or meditation, spirituality also develops during times of reverence and introspection.

Your relationship with your spiritual connection is just as important as the other relationships in your life. It, too, requires your time and attention. Many people are beginning to distinguish between being "spiritual" and being "religious." The spiritual person tends to rely on the internal process while the religious person tends to rely on the external process. The remarkable thing about spirituality is that there is not a right or a wrong practice. For some people, the external process provides the needed structure upon which they can then build their own spiritual practices. However, spirituality goes beyond a physical place. It is more than a particular building, structure, or place where people worship and pay homage to their spiritual connection. True spirituality is unique to each person. Your spiritual beliefs are as distinct and personal as your given name. Therefore, an entire congregation of people can be seated in the same building and share similar as well as distinctive beliefs. Each person brings his or her internal experience and personal perspective into that place of worship or prayerful community. No two people are the same. We all look different, act different, and have different preferences for things. Celebrate your uniqueness. Accept your differences. Customize your spirituality to reflect your beliefs and practices.

Segregation continues to exist between many religions. These are walls that are created by fear. Many religious organizations are threatened by the existence of other religious organizations. Segregation was never God's intention. Spirituality is personal, and therefore does not include judging one's beliefs as correct and another is as incorrect.

Spirituality is like a tree with many branches. The roots and the trunk of the tree support the growth of many different branches. However, the root system and the source of supply is the same. The branches represent the different beliefs and religions, which have grown from the nourishment of the roots. When you look at the beauty of a tree, you recognize that the branches are distinct. The branches do not need to be perfect to receive nourishment. Yet each branch contributes in its own way to the beauty and life of the tree.

Some people will tell you that they do not have to go to church to believe in God. That is, of course, true. However, attendance and participation in a church or synagogue is a means through which a person practices his or her spirituality. How do you practice your spirituality? What is your relationship with your spiritual connection or Higher Power? Is it a relationship like a friendship, in which there is consistent contact, or is it a relationship based solely on need? For instance, when I need you, I will call you, or when I am disappointed or angry, I will let you know. A relationship is a relationship, and therefore it is necessary to have an ongoing and consistent relationship with your chosen spiritual connection.

Create the necessary time in your day or week to get quiet and still. Realize the benefits of such an important practice. This is the foundation from which the practice of meditation develops. Simple meditation is nothing more than being quiet and still. In doing so, you create an opportunity for divine wisdom to inform and guide you. Cultivate this important relationship. Your good depends on it.

Take out a pen and paper and begin your own spiritual journey. Start from wherever you are now. Write down your doubts and your fears. Write down your current beliefs. Continue this process by writing about the spiritual beliefs of your family as you were growing up.

How was spirituality viewed and expressed (or not expressed) in your family?
What was encouraged or discouraged regarding spiritual beliefs?
Did your family go to church? If so, where did you attend, and how often?
What was your understanding about such a practice?
Did your parents share the same spiritual beliefs?
Did you say prayers?
Were you encouraged to ask for God's help during times of crisis or need?
What, if anything, were you taught about God?

Allow your memory to flow as you write. Do not limit yourself or your time. This is a wonderful exercise of getting to know yourself and how you may have inherited some beliefs or practices.
Do any of those beliefs continue to hold true for you today?

Who or what do you believe is responsible for the good in your life? What is your belief about where you came from when you were born on this earth? Where will you go, if anywhere, when you leave this earth?

Develop your own truths. You may find yourself identifying with a particular religion or organization. You may also borrow from various religions to create your own spiritual beliefs and practices.

Spirituality provides direction and perspective. Its gifts include inner peace, happiness, and fulfillment. In addition, spirituality has a significant role in prosperity. Prosperity includes the belief that someone always takes care of you. Someone is looking out for you. Someone cares. Your spiritual connection has proven repeatedly that you are cared for. Look around you and see how the Universe takes care of things such as the earth, the birds, and the trees. The Universe does indeed provide for your every need. It is your feelings of fear and lack that get in the way of simply allowing that to happen.

Trust is the answer to life's many questions.

- ❖ What am I going to do? Trust.
- ❖ Will I get there on time? Trust.
- ❖ Will I be okay? Trust.
- ❖ How will I know what to do? Trust.
- ❖ Will I have what I need? Trust.
- ❖ Will I have enough money? Trust.
- ❖ Will they be there when I arrive? Trust.
- ❖ Will I have an enjoyable time? Trust.

Prosperity builds on the acceptance that someone else is in control of the outcomes and circumstances of your life. Therefore, it is necessary to integrate spirituality into your daily life. Spirituality enables you to trust, and trust produces positive experiences and outcomes.

Remain connected to your spiritual source and know that you will always have exactly what you need. Stop struggling with unnecessary hardship. Instead, develop or strengthen your relationship with your spiritual connection through prayer, meditation, and reflection. Meditation will help you to surrender the fear and embrace trust. You can "let go and let God." When you choose to trust, you also choose to surrender the struggle.

Vicky decided to host a fashion show presenting a particular line of clothes that she liked. She saw it as an opportunity to see the clothes and to get together with friends. As the date approached, many of her invited guests called to inform her that they would not be able to attend. Rather than feeling afraid that no one would come, Vicky chose to "let go and let God." She simply decided to trust rather than worry. Thus, she accepted that whatever the outcome, it was the right outcome. The day arrived and the show was a success. She enjoyed the company of friends and even received free clothes for being the host.

The key to experiencing the good life is to let go of expected outcomes. We are given numerous opportunities to choose either fear or trust, and most of us choose fear. We become afraid when things do not go as expected. We worry when the check is not in the mail or there is a threat of a layoff. We fear when the car does not start, or our teenager is late for curfew. We want control over our life experiences, even when they are impossible to control. To trust the process is to let things flow as they will. Do not stand in the way and impede the process. Where fear blocks the flow, trust moves with the flow.

We are conditioned to react with fear, rather than with trust. Yet, it is trust that leads to prosperity. Trust enables you to be guided. When you trust, you land where you are supposed to land. Allow yourself to be guided like a raft on the river. Let go of the fear. Let go of the need to control or manipulate the outcome. Trust. If something does not seem to be working out the way you had planned, it is working out the way it is supposed to work out.

*Trust the process.*

Life is a process. Become acquainted with trusting the process. Let go and put complete trust in the Universe that what is happening is exactly what is supposed to happen.

A few years ago, I had the incredible privilege of going on a Native American vision quest. Although I was terrified, I was willing to experience this ritual. I wanted to be able to fully trust that God takes care of me, and this seemed like the ultimate test. The vision quest included being alone in the Arizona desert for two days and two nights without food or water. It would simply be me, God, and the wildlife that lives in the desert. So, I packed my trust (as well as a few items I sneaked in, such as sunscreen) and moved toward this experience of a lifetime. However, when I arrived in Arizona the outcome was not as I had anticipated. I was blessed with my monthly "friend," which the Native Americans refer to as "moon-time." As a result, I was told that I would not be able to go out on to the land as I had intended. I was told that a woman's moon-time is a time of reverence. It is a time of reflection and going within. It is not a time for suffering. Therefore, I would experience a different version of the vision quest in the "moon lodge." This became an entirely unique experience for me, but one that has dramatically changed my life. It truly taught me to trust, albeit in an unusual way.

This incredible experience has had lasting effects on my everyday life. The first valuable lesson from this experience was that I no longer had to struggle. I became aware of the degree to which I had created my own struggle. I had convinced myself that struggle was an integral part of growing. After all, "No pain, No gain." This process taught me that I could get my needs met without the struggle, without the sacrifice. I learned that I could surrender the struggle by being more trustful.

The second lesson from this experience was that I could stop doing and start being. My biggest concern about participating in the vision quest (other than seeing a snake) was that I would not have enough to do out on the land. How was I going to occupy my time? I am one of those people who need to be doing something constantly. I love to multi-task. I tend to read several books at the same time. I have various craft projects ready to work on. I create a life in which there is always something to do. I do not want to be bored. Just as we are taught how to do, it is sometimes necessary to be taught how *not* to do. And of course, I tried to do things during my quest in the moon lodge. I attempted to say the rosary, and then lost the rosary beads. I tried to busy myself by making "prayer ties," but they became severely tangled. I eventually surrendered to the realization that I was not supposed to do anything. It became a turning point for me in which I was finally able to let go and let God. I accepted that the outcome was not in my hands. I remembered that it is "Thy will be done," not "My will be done." Perhaps, I can save you the experience of the Moon Lodge although, it is worth doing yourself someday. Surrender the struggle. Swim with the current rather than against it. You will quickly discover how much easier life is.

*You are always in the right place at the right time.*

The Universe guides your everyday life experiences, and as such, you are exactly where you are supposed to be. Yet you tend to fight that fact. You feel like you miss opportunities and regret choices you made or did not make. Again, your focus is on what you have missed, rather than what you are experiencing. Trust the process of life. You arrive when you are supposed to arrive. You work where you are supposed to work. You live where you are supposed to live. You are exactly where you are supposed to be right now in your life. Until otherwise informed, enjoy where you are in your life.

There will be signs when changes are on the horizon. There is a layoff at your job, or a friend invites you to go into business with him or her. The signs will come. You will identify them by their timeliness and by the ease with which they integrate into your life. Until then, you are exactly where you are supposed to be.

For example, if you miss a connecting flight, accept that you were not meant to be on that plane. In trusting that your needs are always met, you simply accept the Universe's alternate plans. Move forward toward whatever experiences await you. Accept that there is a Divine Plan regarding your life. Stop forcing the outcome. Relax. When events in your life take an unusual twist, recognize the humor in it. There is humor, you know. The Universe can be a prankster at times. It is okay. Your needs will be met.

*God is in the details.*

Your spiritual connection is your unlimited supply of good. The Universe provides you with all that you need. When you live in trust, the most amazing things occur as you move through your daily life. Some people call these events miracles. Your life consists of many miracles. Some prefer to call this phenomenon synchronicity. It is when two or more events occur at the same time. For example, the phone rings as you were thinking of the person who telephones. Or you walk into the store and the item you need is half price. Is it coincidence? Or is someone looking out for you? Synchronicity is recognizing that nothing that occurs in your life is simply coincidence.

*The Universe is always working with you and for you.*

Those who dismiss the idea of coincidence embrace the idea of "Divine Intervention." This is the belief that the Universe is in control, guiding and directing you. Again, when you permit yourself to be guided, amazing things occur without reasonable explanation.

> Wayne arrived at a local restaurant for dinner. As he walked in the door there were friends there whom he had not seen in a long time. These friends lived an hour away and had decided to take a drive and have dinner. They were all pleasantly surprised to see one another and asked the host to seat them together. They had dinner together and caught up on their lives.

Divine Intervention is an integral part of adhering to a spiritual process, but unfortunately, when something good happens in our lives, we attribute this good fortune to "luck." We hear ourselves saying such things as, "I was lucky," "As luck would have it," or, "It's just luck." Luck is merely the skeptic's term for God's grace. When good things happen, it is by God's grace and his love for us. It is often the unexpected, but appreciated, thing that went well, arrived on time, and was there when you needed it. God's grace always comes at the right time. As you recognize the existence of God's grace, you will also recognize the frequency in which miracles occur in your life.

Remember that it is not you that support the root,
but the root that supports you.

--Romans 11:18

Trust is the foundation from which you manifest your desires. It is with trust that the closest parking space becomes available, the perfect dress to wear appears in your closet, the clothes are dry, the babysitter is available, and the car has gas. Trust.

When in doubt, trust. When afraid, trust. Move forward on your Divine Path, trusting that you are safe. With practice and persistence, all anxiety will fade from your life. Your good will begin to find its way to you. You meet the most wonderful people, your needs are met, and your experiences are rewarding. You engage in life, laughing and smiling more. Trust makes the colors of your life vibrant. Experience the joy and peace of mind that trust brings to your life.


If you have faith the size of a mustard seed, you will say to this mountain, "Move from here to there," and it will move; and nothing will be impossible for you.

--Matthew 17:20

# Chapter 5

## Order in the House and in Your Life

People can be divided into three groups; those who make things
happen, those who watch things happen, and those who
wonder what happened.

Nicholas Murray Butler

Order attracts prosperity. If you want prosperity, you will need to learn
to live with order rather than chaos. Order includes everything from
how you conduct your daily affairs to the organization of your home and
financial matters. It prevails in your home, your office, and your life.
Everything has its place and can easily be found in its proper place.

Order promotes harmony. When things are in order, you feel less
anxious and frustrated. Order feels good. The problem, of course, is that
there does not seem to be the time necessary to create order. Although
you would enjoy having things in order, your life is busy and hectic. You
go to work, take care of your children, and in the time remaining, you
try to maintain your home. It is hard enough to accomplish the basics—

cooking the meals, doing the laundry, mowing the lawn, and so on. But just suppose you had plenty of time to get things in order. Would having order be important to you? Imagine how it would feel to come home from work and have a clean and organized house. There is room on the kitchen counter to prepare dinner. The dining room table is free of clutter and ready to be set. Order makes it possible to do what you need to do without having to first get organized. Order is organized living.

*Order simplifies your life.*

Order is not to be mistaken for perfectionism. Avoid the mistaken belief that when all is in order, all is perfect. It is unreasonable to expect every drawer, closet, and desk to be perfect. Things just need to be in order. There is a difference. Order brings simplicity. Order brings comfort and serenity. It allows you to find things easily, and therefore makes life a little easier. Perfectionism, on the other hand, is related to feeling inadequate. The person who does not feel good enough or smart enough craves perfection. You do not need things to be perfect in your life. You only need things to be in order.

Order is necessary in life. It prevents confusion and chaos. Imagine what life would be like without traffic lights and stop signs on the streets and intersections. Cars would be running into one another everywhere, and would get stuck in pileups, unable to move in any direction. Although it may be as fun as being on an amusement park ride, it would not be so much fun to experience on your way to work. Rules and regulations provide order. You may not always like the rules, but you need them. Order takes the struggle out of life. Order makes life simple.

The problem with creating order, however, has less to do with time and more to do with the amount of stuff you own. Society tends to define success by material wealth and possessions. "The person with the most toys wins." Material possessions can create the appearance of success and prosperity. For many people it is merely an illusion and should not be mistaken as true prosperity. The ego is known for wanting without having the means or the resources for having. People feel more secure with the more things that they have. Most people have more stuff than they need. The more stuff you have, the greater the chaos in your life. The more things that you accumulate, the less storage space you have. The more stuff you have, the longer it takes to find what you need.

*The more you have, the less order there is.*

The only way to achieve order is to engage in the cleaning-out process. It is through this cleaning-out process that you make room for your desired good. You create the physical space to have the things that you genuinely want in your life. Be willing to create an open space in your life, in your home, and in your closet to invite the good to come. Fill your cupboards, drawers, and closets with only the things that you genuinely want. Do not settle for less than what is desired and be willing to wait for what you want. Spring clean all year round. You must continually create the room for your desired good. Although some people love to spring clean, most people merely enjoy the feelings that accompany a clean and organized home.

*Order saves time.*

When things are in order, you add time to your busy schedule. Consider how much time is wasted looking for something you need to do something else. "Where are the scissors?" "Where are the car keys?" "Where is the permission slip?" Without order, it takes longer to do even the most trivial tasks, and this drains your emotional energy. Many people become angry and frustrated when they cannot find a desired item. They blame family members for not putting the item back where it belongs. It causes loved ones to exchange hurtful words and defensive reactions. And all because the Scotch tape is not in the drawer!

Order makes life easier and puts fewer demands on your time and energy. How many times have you raced out to purchase an item that you already own but cannot seem to find? It seems easier to go out and buy another one than to deal with having to waste time searching for it. Some people may even purchase items in bulk to increase the odds of having the item when they need it. This compensation for a lack of order does not save money. It costs more money.

Look at your closets, your cupboards, and your drawers. What is all that stuff in there that you have not used in months or even years? Does that old battery even work? Do you really use all those pens? Can you easily find what you need without sifting through assorted items that you do not use? When you discover some lost treasure, do you hear yourself saying, "Wow, I was looking for that," or "I knew I had one of these"?

Do you have a "junk drawer" in your home? My family kept one in the kitchen throughout my childhood years. This was the drawer where you could find anything—tools, rubber bands, thumbtacks, and so on. If you were looking for something, you were told to "look in the junk drawer." The term junk drawer implies that you need a place to keep your junk. If you are calling the items "junk," chances are you do not need these things. Alas, get rid of the junk. Make room in your life for what you need and want.

Have you looked in your closets lately? When was the last time you cleaned out your closets and got rid of clothes that you do not like or that no longer fit properly? Donate the clothes that you do not wear, and even those clothes that you hope to "fit into someday." If you are hoping to lose weight, choose a few items of the desired size and give the rest away. Styles change, and when you lose weight, you will want to wear the latest style. Discard clothes that are worn or out of style. Fill your closets only with clothes that you absolutely love, and give the rest to a charity, a friend, or a family member. Just think about how much easier it will be to choose your clothes for work tomorrow.

Paper is another obstacle to achieving order in our lives. Our daily lives are inundated with paper—mail, catalogues, newspapers, and advertisements. We accumulate stacks of paper in our homes and offices, and then the papers need to be sorted, organized, and put in a proper place. Chances are good that you have more papers than you have places for them. Therefore, papers collect in boxes, drawers, and on the kitchen table or kitchen counter. They seem to sit there for days, weeks, or even months. You just move the pile from one place to another as you tell yourself that you "have to go through this." Make your life simpler. Discard or file these miscellaneous papers as they arrive. Go through your mail in the company of a wastebasket. By doing this, the unnecessary papers will not find their way into the stagnant piles, and the piles you do have will be smaller and feel less overwhelming. You might even say, "Wow, there is not that much here. I can take care of this right now and have it done." Of course, filing papers is easier when you have the available space, so go through your file cabinet and throw away papers that are years old.

*Move those papers.*

Discard the old bills and the out-of-date policies. Keep these things only if you still may need them. Get rid of the warranties on things that you sold at a yard sale several years ago. Pull out the expired rabies certificates. It is not necessary to hold on to things indefinitely. It is unlikely that there will be a need for your electric bill that was paid five years ago. Most papers are organized simply by throwing them away. Fewer papers will make your life easier and more manageable. It will be easy to locate last year's taxes when requested by a bank or creditor.

Monthly bills also need to be in order. Although many people are discovering the ease of electronic bill paying and auto-payment, some people prefer to receive the paper bills. If this, is you, do you keep your bills neat and organized? Or are they thrown in a pile somewhere? Bills need to be easy to find. They need to be organized in a way that allows you to know what is due, the amount due, and the due date. Good record keeping is essential to a prosperous life. Throw away the advertisements that accompany the bills. Discard the used envelopes. You only need the bill and the envelope in which to mail it. You need to keep the flow of papers moving so you do not block your prosperity. Do not let things sit idle. In doing so, your good also sits idle in the invisible sphere. Keep things circulating and experience how quickly your dreams manifest on the visible plane.

*Order needs to be everywhere.*

When was the last time you defrosted your freezer? Do you even know what you have in there? Can you locate what you need, or do you have to move items to find what you are looking for? Refrigerators and freezers need order, too. They easily become cluttered with things you do not like or have not used in a long time.

When was the last time you cleaned out the family medicine cabinet? Are there pharmaceutical supplies and prescriptions that you do not recognize because they have been there for so long? Keep only a small quantity of what you need. Do not invite illness into your life by being overly prepared for it. If you do become sick, trust that you will have what you need or be able to purchase what you need. Medications get old and lose their effectiveness. Therefore, to "have it on hand" does not necessarily mean that you will have what you need.

Take the time to go through your house one room at a time. Clean out your basement, your attic, and your garage. Clean out the laundry room. Are there things on the floor? Prosperity needs a clean path to your life. Clean out the boxes that have yet to be unpacked since you moved into your new home It is time to discard or donate. Is it necessary to keep forty-two empty gift boxes? You can always get more. When you hold on to things, you are inadvertently telling the Universe that there is lack and limitation in your life. You live in fear. Consequently, you will continue to attract lack and limitation. Learn to have what you need.

*Live in order.*

Organize your storage room. Throw away things that are broken. Get rid of the broken toaster and the ice cream machine you never used. In doing so, you tell the Universe that you are not willing to have things that are broken and unusable. Free yourself and your home of the many things that you have not used in years. Keep only what is sentimental or irreplaceable. Try not to confuse sentiment with fear. If something is sentimental, it is of value to you and is not replaceable. Fear convinces you that you will not have what you need. Therefore, you hold on to things that you do not like, use, or enjoy. By holding on, you block the channel of having what you genuinely want. Stop stuffing your closets and drawers with things for which you have little or no use, and instead create space for what you really want to have.

*Learn to live in a clutter-free environment.*

If you do not particularly like housecleaning, consider hiring someone who cleans well and can do it for you. It does not matter how your house becomes clean and organized, as long as it does.

> Mark and Jody had a beautiful home. Yet they both worked full-time and had a one-year-old son. They did not have the time to clean their home. After many arguments regarding the appearance of the house, they decided to call and see how much a housekeeping service would cost. They were pleasantly surprised. They chose to pay someone to clean their house each week. The arguments ceased and they were able to enjoy precious time together as a family.

Get your house and affairs in order and be diligent about keeping them in order. Although it is easy for things to get cluttered, it takes significantly more time to get things back in order. Invest the time and energy it takes to keep things organized. It feels good. It gives your prosperity an uncluttered path into your life. Order creates a clear path to the manifestation of your dreams and desires.

*Keep your car neat and clean.*

And then there is the car. Have you looked in your car lately? Is it clean and orderly, or is it cluttered with stuff? Do you use your car as if it were an additional storage unit? Could you live out of your car if you had to? The trunk can contain anything from extra clothes and sweatshirts to towels and wrapping paper. But could you find a flashlight if you needed one? Again, the trunk of the car is a place where you may keep more things than you need.

Have you looked in the glove box lately? Could an actual pair of gloves fit into your glove box? This is usually the storage place for all the small miscellaneous items found on the floor and under the seats. "Oh, just put it in the glove box." The glove box is another place where you can count on finding some long-lost items. It could be a problem on those rare occasions when you are asked to locate the insurance card and car registration. Now, where would you have put that?!

Believe it or not, your vehicle needs to be in order as well. Do not leave things on the seat for days and weeks at a time. Things do not belong in your car for lengthy periods of time. Bring these things into your house or office or drop them off where they belong.

Clean out the trunk. Organize the tools and discard anything that is not important to the operation and safety of the vehicle. Keep the necessary things such as appropriate tools, a flashlight, a jack, a spare tire, and so on. Do not use the trunk of your car for extra storage space. The car trunk is a temporary place for things that are being transported from one place to another. Things are not meant to be in there permanently.

Clean and organize your office. Maintain a neat and organized desk. Do not be afraid to throw out paper that has gathered on your desk; again, we tend to keep papers longer than necessary. This, of course, creates clutter and confusion. "Didn't I already do this?" "I wonder if I mailed that already." Do not leave papers lying around for you to look at repeatedly. Get in the habit of handling papers purposefully—organize the papers, then file or discard them.

Throw out the used post-it notes and the pieces of scrap paper. Clean off and dust your computer. Update and organize your equipment to enhance efficiency and productivity. A cluttered desk drains the energy necessary for maximum productivity. Clutter overwhelms the mind.

Make room for your work. Discard the old telephone messages and memos. Throw out the highlighters and pens that no longer work. Keep your drawers and files neat and your pencils sharpened. Let your workspace speak of success, not failure. Create an atmosphere that welcomes productivity and vitalizes your energy.

*Order enhances your emotional health.*

Clients who suffer from depression are often advised to choose one task that puts some order into their lives. The results are astounding. They typically report feeling better as their lives become orderly. Order influences your emotions. Clutter and chaos distract you and prevent you from feeling centered and grounded. Your physical world is connected to your inner world (thoughts, feelings, and beliefs). A cluttered physical space tends to create a cluttered and often overwhelming emotional and mental existence.

Look around you now. Is there one thing that you can pick up, put away, or put in order? Perhaps it is something simple, like hanging up a freshly laundered skirt or putting a document in the file cabinet. Take a moment now to put something around you in its proper place. How does it feel to have done that? Now, consider how much time it took you to put that one item away. It does not take a significant amount of time to put things in order. You just anticipate that it will. You make it out to be such a dreadful task. Therefore, you avoid it until it stirs you up internally. Consequently, you feel irritated and frustrated, instead of carefree and content.

When your space is cluttered, you are not sure where to begin organizing, and wonder if the project will ever end. Avoid thinking or saying, "I don't know where to start." It does not matter. Just start. Where you are sitting or standing now is a good place to start. Keep it simple. Do not be sabotaged by feeling overwhelmed. Instead, establish a visual boundary, such as a certain space (kitchen counter) or specific room (bathroom). By having this boundary, you can clearly see the end. It gives you a needed sense of completion and accomplishment. When the counter is clean, you have accomplished what you set out to do. All that is left is to sit back and appreciate your work.

Be persistent. Do not give into feelings of frustration and discouragement. It is easy to feel frustrated when the other members of your household undo what you have already done. You adopt the pessimistic belief of "Why bother, it is only going to be messed up again soon." This is not prosperity thinking. Prosperity requires persistence. You need to make a commitment to preserve order regardless of how long it lasts. Just because you will need to make your bed tomorrow does not mean it should not be made today. Prosperity is living in the now. What you accomplish now is what matters!

Teach your children and your spouse how to maintain and live-in order. Teach them the benefits of order and be willing to allow for the natural consequences that arise from a lack of order. That is, try not to rescue them the next time they cannot locate a desired item that they are responsible for (shoes, ties, keys, backpack, and so on). It is possible to teach order and responsibility without blame or shame. Simply respond to their pleas for help with, "Let's see, I last saw you with them in the living room." Teach responsibility through encouragement rather than shame. "Where do you want to put these so that you can easily find them later?" Avoid jumping in and saving the day. This can be difficult to do, especially when your husband is yelling that he cannot find his wallet and he is late for work. Many people make changes only after the situation is unbearable and they are at their wit's end. Allow your family to experience the frustration that accompanies a lack of order. As they say, "Experience is the best teacher." After several experiences of utter frustration, they will either put things where they belong or be destined to lead a chaotic lifestyle. After all, you will not be able to follow them throughout their lives, helping them to find their belongings. Eventually they will have to develop their own system of organization. Of course, there are people who prefer things to be out of order. For them, chaos is familiar. There is a sense of comfort that comes from what is already known. However, prosperity has a tough time finding its way through chaos and confusion.

Order serves two purposes. First, it makes life easier. Life is simpler when you can find what you need. Second, it creates an open channel for you to receive good into your life. Order permits things to flow smoothly into your life and affairs. However, it is necessary to create the space for the things that you really want. That is, you need to make room for your good to arrive.

Catherine Ponder, author of Dynamic Laws of Prosperity, refers to this concept as the "vacuum law of prosperity." It refers specifically to cleaning out the old, the unused, and often the unnecessary things of your life, so you can create room for what you genuinely want.

*Make room for your desired good.*

Create the space for whatever you want to attract into your life, whether it is a larger dining room table or a new computer. Start with letting go of what you have so you can make the space for what you desire. By doing so you communicate to the Universe your readiness to receive what you want. Of course, this may mean that the space is empty for a while. Many people feel uncomfortable with open space, so they tend to hold on to what they have until they can get what they want.

Release those things that no longer serve a purpose for you. Instead of letting them sit idle, give them to someone who can use and appreciate them. Letting go of the old creates room for the new. Send out the old and undesirable into the Universe with love and kindness, knowing that your true desires are coming forth in exactly the right time. Release with gratitude all possessions that are no longer used or needed. Learn to let go and to simplify. Embrace the trust that you always have what you need. Learn to have only what you need and to love what you have.

*Keep your money and all financial affairs in order.*

The need for order does not only apply to your homes and offices, but to your money and other financial affairs as well. It is essential to identify how you physically treat money in your life. Where do you keep your cash? Do you keep it crumpled in your pocket? Do you throw change into the bottom of your purse? Is your money separated and kept in various places like your wallet, your coat pocket, your dresser, and your car? In other words, do you know where your money is? Do you treat the money you have with respect? The way in which you treat and care for your money is significant if you want to achieve a life of prosperity and abundance. It is your treatment of money that often speaks of your true thoughts and feelings about money. There are very few people who fold their dollar bills neatly and keep their money and change in their wallets and purses.

There are people reluctant to give up their money. There are people who overpay and underpay for services and goods. Folded-up bills and checks are pulled out of some unexpected places such as bras, shoes, and socks.

Joan did not like to carry a purse. As a child growing up in New York City she learned to carry money in her shoe. It was something she preferred to do. One day she went to pay for groceries, and the cashier discovered a hole in the bill, which was caused by her foot rubbing against it. She was delayed for questions, as the store mistakenly believed that her money was counterfeit.

This mistreatment of cash inadvertently communicates disrespect for money. It is as if the money means nothing and is worthless to you. Look at what you are communicating about money when you handle it poorly.

- I have this money, but it does not mean anything.
- So what? Who cares? I should not have it anyway.
- Look, I cannot even be responsible for it. I cannot take care of it.
- I do not know how much I have, and it does not really matter.
- It is only money. It is worthless.

When you mistreat your money, it is likely to resist you, meaning that your money is not there when you need it. It slips away faster. Many people inadvertently send it away because of feeling uncomfortable with it or unworthy of it. When you are scared or reluctant to manage your money, you are more susceptible to throwing it away. We are a society accustomed to "throwing change." We throw it on the floor, we throw it into wells and fountains, and we drop it into buckets and containers. When you treat money in this manner, you are communicating its lack of value and significance in your life. Yet we all need enough of it to have the things we most desire.

Amy was on vacation with friends in Sedona, Arizona. Upon returning to their parked rental car, they discovered that they had forgotten to lock the doors. Amy felt nervous and checked for her money, which she had left in the car. She could not find it. She convinced herself that someone had taken her six hundred dollars in cash. Her friends continued to reassure her that the money was there, and that it had only been temporarily misplaced. Sometime later in the day, Amy discovered the cash, which was loose in her bag.

Money can repel you. You lose money. You drop money. It is easy to misplace or lose when you put it in arbitrary places. Money belongs in wallets. If you keep your money in your wallet, you will always know where to find it. A fear of being robbed leads some people to place their money in their socks and shoes, or wherever they think their money will be safe. To prevent a potential robber from stealing their money, they place it in a "safe place," but sometimes they forget where this place is. Treat your money well. Purchase a nice wallet and keep your cash organized inside of it.

*Wallets are meant to carry cash.*

Your wallet is not a portable filing cabinet. Remove all the miscellaneous papers such as receipts, business cards, telephone numbers, and so on, as they only serve to monopolize the space and prevent the attraction of money. Find another appropriate place for them. Your wallet needs order, much like all the other areas of your life. Keep your wallet free of clutter, as clutter only produces more clutter and prevents you from attracting what you really want to have in your wallet (and what your wallet is intended to carry: cash!).

*Keep some amount of cash in your wallet as a magnet*
*to attract additional money.*

Organize the money in your wallet. Keep the bills neatly stored in your wallet. Sarah Ban Breathnach, the author of Simple Abundance, suggests that you have the back of the bills facing you when placing them in your wallet or paying someone. In doing so, you can easily see those familiar words that are printed on every bill: "In God We Trust." This reminds us of our need to trust in the Higher Power that all our financial needs are always met. God is the source of our infinite supply of prosperity and abundance.

Money needs to be treated with respect. Money is energy, and therefore needs to be valued and appreciated if you want to have the financial means to meet all your needs. A healthy relationship with money consists of appreciating and valuing it, without worshipping it. It was never intended for money to dominate life. Money is to be had, and not to be feared. Yet many people use money as a premise for their decisions. If they perceive that money is there, they decide that they can do "it" (travel, make purchases, retire, and so on). If they perceive that the money is not there, then they decide that they cannot do it.

Control your money rather than letting it control you. Keep track of it without being consumed by how much you have or do not have. Be consciously aware of when and how you spend your money. It is only by paying attention to money that you gain more of it.

If you are in a relationship with another, work together to financially grow and prosper. Financial success comes more quickly when couples are working together. Couples need to share equally in their management of their financial affairs. If both are aware of the bottom line, then both are working to improve or enhance their present financial situation. Do not hide bills and purchases from your spouse. To keep things from another is to battle the feelings of shame, fear, and unworthiness, all of which repel prosperity. Be in your integrity by acting in a way that is honest and truthful.

So, now that your house, office, and financial affairs are beginning to take shape, it is time to make sure that your clothing and outward appearance speak of prosperity. "Dress the part." Allow your physical appearance to demonstrate your belief in prosperity and abundance.

*Dress for success.*

Your appearance illustrates to others how you expect to be treated. When a man goes to court dressed in a suit and tie, he is presenting a professional image. He intends to earn the respect of the court. Respect and credibility are gained when you appear prosperous and successful. This is the same reason that you dress nicely for a job interview. You "dress to impress."

Immediate assumptions are made about people on the mere basis of what is observed. Others make assumptions about you based on the clothes you wear, the car you drive, and the home in which you live. Therefore, your outward appearance is important and needs to reflect the prosperous lifestyle you desire to live. To dress in a professional manner also illustrates personal esteem. Keep your clothes neat and pressed. And since your closet only contains clothes that fit well and look good on you, it is easy to dress nicely.

It is necessary to create order in all aspects of your life. Take out the thoughts notebook that was discussed in chapter 3. Write down the things that you want to get in order.

The following is a helpful guide for maintaining order in your life:

- If it is broken, throw it out.
- If it is dirty, clean it.
- If it is wrinkled, straighten it.
- If you drop it, pick it up.
- If you spilled it, wipe it up.
- If you broke it, fix it, or replace it.
- If you borrowed it, return it.
- If you took it out, put it back.
- If you bought it, use it, or get rid of it.
- If you said you would do it, do it.

*Order enriches your life.*

Life is simpler when there is order. When things are in order, you always have what you need. In addition, you also know what you do and do not have. Order provides you with more of the things you do want, including more money and time. Order creates an open channel for a continuous flow of good things and good experiences in your life. When there is order, all is good.

Make a commitment to yourself today to invite more order into your life. Be willing to assign specific places to the stuff in your life. Have a yard sale and liberate yourself from the many things that you do not want or have not used in a long time. Give your unused items to those who will use them. Make regular donations to local charities.

Living in order is an ongoing process. Do not despair. Just put something in order today and you will have begun the process. Life feels so wonderful and fulfilling when there is harmony and order. Life is more relaxing and enjoyable. With order, all is well. You look good, your car is clean, your home is orderly, and your wallet carries cash rather than receipts. You are prosperous! Life is simple. Life is good.

Ellen Peterson

# Chapter 6

## Integrity: The Challenge to Do What Is Right

The soul is dyed the color of its thoughts. The content of your character is your choice. Day by day, what you choose, what you think, and what you do is who you become. Your integrity is your destiny. It is the light that guides your way.

-- Heraclitus, Greek Poet, Philosopher

Integrity. Integrity is a word frequently used in conversations with others. Many people share their personal values regarding integrity and hold others accountable for being in their integrity. Integrity implies something of significant importance. It is a respected value. Therefore, most people are quick to say that they have integrity without really considering the meaning of the word. Most people simply define integrity as "being a good person." The dictionary defines integrity as "the quality or state of being of sound moral principle; uprightness, honesty, and sincerity" (Webster's Deluxe Unabridged Dictionary). How do you define integrity?

Integrity is a value that is taught to you. Integrity was instilled in me at the mere age of five. While in a convenience store with my mother, I noticed a box of Bazooka bubble gum that was located on a shelf under the cashier counter. As my mother paid for items, I innocently put a few pieces of gum in my pocket and unwrapped one piece and put it in my mouth. As we walked out of the store, my mother looked at me curiously and asked me what was in my mouth. Not knowing what I had done, I told her that it was a piece of gum. She asked me where I got it and I truthfully told her, "At the store." She marched me back into the store and made me apologize to the clerk, return what I had taken, and pay for what I had eaten. Despite the feeling of humiliation, I realized then the difference between right and wrong. I had learned the important lesson of integrity.

Integrity is the rulebook of life. However, this important rulebook of life is too often ignored, misinterpreted, or thrown out entirely. In fact, Ann Landers, an American advice columnist, made a successful living from advising people on how to honor their integrity by doing the "right thing." Most people feel lost regarding integrity issues. They are aware of the word but lack the knowledge of how to apply this word to their everyday living.

*Your integrity is challenged daily.*

Integrity is being honest and forthright. Integrity is being accountable for your thoughts, your feelings, and your actions. Are you 100 percent honest 100 percent of the time? Okay, so you do not steal. You do not try to make money out of your basement. You have never been in jail. You have never physically assaulted or abused anyone. You work for a living. Is that enough? Most people are aware of the obvious violations of integrity. However, there are more subtle ways in which people step out of their integrity, and often without conscious awareness.

Violations of integrity usually accompany the feeling of getting away with something. It is pushing the speed limit when there is not a police car in sight. It is feeling relieved when you were not "caught" copying personal invitations on the company copier. It is feeling delighted when the cashier accidentally overlooked an item in your shopping cart. It is feeling lucky to mistakenly receive an extra five dollars in change.

Integrity is being honest and doing what is right, particularly when no one else makes you accountable. Integrity is demonstrated through your everyday decisions and actions. Have you ever told a telemarketer that you are not home, when indeed you are the one speaking on the phone? It may seem easier to tell a small "white lie" than to have to argue with a stranger during dinner. Lies of any color are not in your integrity. Sure, you can justify your actions. After all, you are having dinner. You do not want to be disturbed, much less tied up on the phone for any length of time.

It is easy to make excuses for decisions that lack integrity. You were late to the meeting, and therefore needed to cut through the parking lot to avoid a long red light. You mailed that bill late because you did not have a chance to write out your bills. You simply forgot that you borrowed money from a colleague for lunch one day. You would have paid her back had you remembered. These situations indeed happen. Despite having a reasonable excuse, your actions take you out of your integrity. In other words, you stepped out of your integrity. The following are other common ways that you step out of your integrity:

- Arriving late or not showing up
- Failure to complete projects
- Talking behind someone's back
- Withholding information; distorting the truth
- Failing to follow through on a commitment or promise
- Parking in a handicapped space
- Taking two spaces in a parking lot
- A cluttered office, home, or car
- Leaving work early without your employer's knowledge
- Taking or using office supplies for personal use
- Not balancing your checkbook
- Not returning telephone calls, faxes, or e-mail messages
- Not opening mail
- Not paying the parking meter
- Not getting things repaired
- Not acknowledging the receipt of a gift
- Not calling to RSVP as the invitation requests
- Not paying people back

• Not returning borrowed items

Until now, you may not have considered how these common experiences reflect your personal integrity. This is not meant to scare you or to shame you, but to simply raise your awareness. There are many subtle violations of integrity.

Another common violation of integrity is the misuse of money. We live in a society in which consumer debt is growing rapidly. Have there been times when you have paid for an item with a credit card knowing that you could not afford to make such a purchase? You wanted the item so badly that you pulled the plastic card from your wallet anyway. Have you had to rely on credit cards to pay your monthly bills because the money was not in the bank? Credit cards are frequently used to temporarily close the gap between a person's fixed income and growing expenses. Although it may now be considered "the American way," credit card usage in this way is a misuse of money.

Suze Orman, author of Courage to be Rich, differentiates between good debt and bad debt. Purchasing a car or taking out a loan for education, business, or home renovations are examples of appropriate debts to have. They entail accruing debt for something of greater value that serves to enhance one's life. However, many people accrue bad debt by (mis)using their credit cards to pay off other credit cards (revolving debt), or by purchasing more of the things they cannot find, cannot use, or have no time to enjoy.

Credit cards give an illusion of money when in fact you are taking out loans when you use them. These loans tend to replace the hope of "saving money for a rainy day," yet you still buy another pair of jeans. "But they're on sale! I will save money!" Again, it is easy to justify your actions. The truth is that these justifications are illogical thoughts under disguise. How can you save money that does not exist?

*Items are on sale every day in every store every week.*

Be kind to yourself and all your tomorrows by cutting up your credit cards. Leave yourself one credit card that gives you something in return (airline tickets, money toward a vehicle, and so on). You only need one credit card.

If you are reluctant to cut up your credit cards, then remove them from your wallet. Do not allow credit cards to tempt you and to disrupt your financial welfare. Put them in a safe place that is not easily accessible. Credit cards are merely loans that must be paid back with accruing interest. As a person of integrity, you pay with cash that you have already earned, cash that is available for this purchase. In turn, you save yourself the unpleasant feelings of guilt, shame, and despair. As a person of integrity, you make conscious decisions about when and how you spend your money.

Bankruptcy is another way in which people sacrifice their integrity. It is most often the result of mismanaging credit and misusing money. The number of bankruptcies has increased with the increase in credit card usage. Bankruptcy opposes prosperity consciousness and is nothing more than a poor attempt to alleviate feelings of impoverishment and hopelessness. Bankruptcy cheats people, and therefore it cheats the Universe. Bankruptcy carries feelings of shame and inadequacy and may leave a person feeling like a failure for years afterward. Sadly, for some people it seems like the only exit.

*Integrity is doing what is right, regardless of the cost or level of inconvenience.*

I once had an interesting dream that gave me a greater understanding of personal integrity. At the time of having this dream, I was interested in purchasing a conversion van for family travel. The dream consisted of me finding such a van. The van was all that I had hoped it would be. It was both sporty and colorful, with a reasonable asking price. However, when I glimpsed through the window of the van, I discovered the interior to be quite alarming. The front seats were atypical for a conversion van, and there were no back seats at all. The interior had garbage strewn all about. I wondered how something that nice on the outside could be such a mess on the inside. The outside should reflect the inside; and this is also true of integrity. Your integrity is obvious to others in all that you say and all that you do. If you said it, you will surely do it.

Integrity is communicating your thoughts and feelings. In doing so, you are not likely to hold a grudge. Grudges are a way in which people avoid direct communication. The holder of a grudge makes other people responsible for his or her feelings. This is a game that has no winners. Furthermore, without the necessary communication, you are not aware of what caused the person to feel or react in such a way. That is his or her well-kept secret. It is as if the person is mad at you for not playing the game right, yet he or she hides the rulebook.

Many times, grudges are accompanied by the infamous "silent treatment." As with grudges, the purpose of the silent treatment is to punish, rather than resolve the issue. These tactics are used when a person is unable to verbally communicate his or her feelings of hurt or anger. Therefore, the person uses behavior to communicate his or her feelings. These unexpressed feelings multiply and eventually turn into resentment. Resentment continues to build even when the original incident has passed, and the specifics can no longer be accurately recalled. Consequently, families are pulled apart and may not speak to one another for years.

RECIPE FOR SILENT TREATMENT

Take one person who has a good memory for bad experiences.
Add in the ability to hold in one's feelings.
Mix gradually with at least one other person who is unaware of the situation.
Stir thoroughly with gossiping to others.
Add a dash of exaggeration for extra flavor.
Bring to a boil.
Let simmer for as long as possible.

*Use words, not behaviors, to communicate with others.*

People are quite adept at using behaviors rather than words to communicate their feelings. They also expect others to understand and interpret their behavior in the way that they intend. This is not possible, of course. Behaviors such as the silent treatment, walking angrily out of a room, or sleeping on the couch are a form of indirect communication. It invites others to make assumptions based entirely on what they see, which can be quite inaccurate. Although your behaviors may complement your words, they do not sufficiently replace your words. Words are needed to communicate feelings.

Have you ever been asked, "What's wrong?" only to respond with, "Nothing"? If you have been asked this question, you are probably a person who uses behaviors to communicate feelings. The person is reading your behavior and determining that something is "wrong" based on a simple observation. To respond with "Nothing" is usually an avoidance tactic. This simple one-word response can be translated many ways. It could mean "You know what's wrong," "You should know what's wrong by now," or "I'm not telling you what's wrong; you have to guess." At times, it can mean "Not now" or "Leave me alone." It is rare that "Nothing" means nothing.

Avoid the temptation to make people guess what you are feeling. Choose words that honestly communicate your thoughts and feelings.

Integrity is completing projects and tasks. Are there things that you have started but have yet to finish? Is the house only partially painted? Is that sweater you have been knitting for months "almost done"? Like many people, you entertain the hope of finishing a project, but rarely get around to doing it. You surrender to the thought that "there is only so much time in a day." Although there are many reasons for not finishing a project, the result is the same, sadly. Incomplete projects lead to feeling defeated and unsuccessful. Yet these negative feelings do not seem to motivate most people to complete the project. Instead, the project lingers over their heads like a black cloud. You know that you must finish it, but you cannot seem to find the time to do it. Therefore, this unfinished business creates a feeling of being overwhelmed and the sense of always having something to do.

> Maureen prides herself on her ability to read several different books at the same time. She has a bookcase over her bed, which is stocked with miscellaneous books, all of which contain bookmarks. She enjoys reading before she falls asleep at night. She simply selects a different book each night. She admits that books sit on the shelf for months until she has the time to read them.

Unfinished books create bookcases that are cluttered with unfinished business. Some people struggle emotionally if they have nothing to do, and therefore they keep a running list of things to do.

Our society admires people who multitask. We believe that there is value in doing two or more things at the same time, so we tell our children to pick up their backpacks as they are lacing their shoes, or to pick up their bath toys while they are brushing their teeth. Although we like to think that this will save time, it rarely does. Multiple tasks increase our level of distraction. We start something new and forget to return to what we were previously working on. Therefore, multiple tasks increase the likelihood that something will be left unfinished.

Incomplete projects invite the Universe to do the same with the delivery of your good. Although your good begins to materialize, it never fully comes in the way you had desired. Your good is preempted. It is delayed or stuck in neutral.

Make your life simpler. Learn to complete one task prior to moving to the next one. If necessary, create a "to complete" list to organize your numerous projects. Completing things feels good. And anything that feels good certainly deserves repeating.

So, pick up that book, needlepoint, or other unfinished project, and work on it until it is complete. You are a person of integrity.

*Keep your commitments, agreements, and appointments.*

Do you have a reputation for arriving late? For instance, the party invitation reads 3:00 p.m. and you casually arrive at 4:00 p.m. Integrity is arriving when you are expected to arrive. Arriving on time is a demonstration of your integrity. It speaks of your respect for other people. A late arrival stalls or disrupts the process. It means that others are forced to wait for you, and therefore others are delayed as well. Discover how good it feels to be on time. Arrive on time and you will eliminate the feelings of embarrassment and shame that accompany tardiness. Give yourself the gift of time. In fact, choose to give yourself "more than enough time." Incorporate extra time into your schedule. Extra time allows for the inconvenience of forgetting something in the house or not finding something immediately and makes life more pleasant and enjoyable. Extra time takes the stress out of living.

Life consists of many commitments, agreements, and appointments. It can be challenging to keep them straight. Calendars, when used consistently, are quite handy. To cancel or simply forget an appointment means that you are violating an agreement. This, of course, means that you are not in your integrity. Although you may have a good reason, you still broke your stated agreement. Good integrity depends on the keeping of agreements, commitments, and appointments. Keep the agreements that you choose to make with others; they can be renegotiated but should never be entirely broken. If you are unsure of being able to keep a commitment that you made, then be honest about that from the beginning by saying something like, "I am not sure I will be available to help you on that day."

A lack of integrity is a significant obstacle to living a happy and prosperous life. It inhibits the good from coming into your life in the way in which you would like it to flow. Consequently, you cheat yourself from having what you truly desire. Set the stage for how you want to be treated by the Universe. Keep your commitments, and the Universe will keep its commitment to you to manifest your needs and desires. So, make that telephone call, send out that bill, take your daughter to the zoo. Keep your promises regardless of how big or small. If you said it, do it. If you signed it, it is your responsibility to live up to the commitment. If others are counting on you, be available.

*Integrity is living consciously.*

Integrity includes being helpful and considerate of others. It is holding the door open for the person behind you. It is extending a hand to someone in need. It is helping a person retrieve his or her lost belongings. It is allowing the person with a few items to go in front of you at the cashier line. It is simply smiling at a stranger who passes you on the sidewalk.

Integrity is being kind and courteous rather than angry and resentful. As an example, take the many people who engage in "road rage." This is a behavior that clearly communicates feelings of impatience, anger, and resentment. And chances are, these feelings go well beyond their time in a car. Driving only provokes the negative feelings, which already exist. What is so difficult about smiling and letting another car go first? In doing so, we are reminded of how the Universe brings forth all that we need and desire. As we allow life to flow easily and without contention, we invite our desires to manifest.

Integrity is being respectful of other people and their property. Take care of other people's belongings. Show respect for their home. Take off your shoes. Use a coaster. Request an ashtray. Inform your host of a breakage or spill. A person of integrity assumes responsibility for his or her actions and apologizes as needed.

Integrity is meeting your responsibilities. Mow the lawn. Get the oil changed in the car. Clean the garage. Vacuum the rug. Pay your bills. Schedule your medical appointments. Return telephone calls. Open your mail. Pay attention to the details of your life.

Tammy and Diane stopped at a rummage sale to see if there was anything of interest to them. Tammy found one pair of designer pants. However, when she did not find anything else of interest, she decided to put the pants back and wait for her friend. The lady at the register stated that they would be closing soon, and that each of them could take a bag and pay a dollar for the entire contents of the bag. Tammy took a bag and continued to look around, but still found only the one pair of pants. Diane, whose bag was half-full, encouraged Tammy to put the pants in her bag, which Tammy did. A few moments later, Tammy turned to Diane and said, "That is not right. It is not in my integrity. I can afford to pay a dollar," and she placed the pants back in her own bag. When she turned around to pay the dollar, she discovered a whole rack of designer pants in her size. She was excited and returned home with five pairs of pants for which she paid one dollar.

Integrity is doing what is right, not out of the fear of a negative consequence, but because it is what you know to be right. To do what you know is not right only cheats the Universe. And when you cheat the Universe, the Universe will cheat you! You may think that no one will notice or care, but the Universe does notice and does care. It observes you as you drop that piece of paper on the ground and look the other way. It is watching when you make the U-turn in a designated No U-turn area. It is watching you nonchalantly step over an empty and discarded paper cup. It watches as you abandon the shopping cart by your car rather than returning it to where it belongs. It is watching you as you judge other people for things you do or have done. It is watching you as you cut in front of people standing in line. It sees you shortchanging the waiter's tip. The Universe is paying attention. It is watching.

*Do your Part!*

Integrity requests your participation in the general good of this planet. Do your part, whether it is picking up a piece of paper that missed the garbage or taking your plate to the kitchen. Pitch in. Volunteer. Give back to the world. Choose to give in some way. In a later chapter you will learn how giving invites prosperity.

In the Native American culture, if you take from the earth, you must give back to the earth. Do your part to nurture and care for the earth, which nourishes and sustains you. Mother Earth, as she is most suitably named, deserves your love and respect. Therefore, be conscious of your actions toward her. Do not throw your cigarette on the ground or out the car window. Do not litter. If you drop a napkin, pick it up. If you see a piece of paper while walking, pick it up and discard it appropriately. To walk past it is to invite the Universe to ignore or walk past your dreams. Do your part. Contribute to the welfare of this planet while also contributing to your own good.

Your contribution does not have to be something extraordinary like finding a cure for AIDS. It can be as simple as picking up your coffee cup or pushing in your chair. Integrity incorporates leaving things ready for the next person to use. So, wipe down the sink, put down the toilet seat, and straighten the hand towel. Get a new roll of toilet paper when necessary and replace the tissue box when it is empty. These are simple things that communicate respect and consideration for other people. Leaving things undone, or for someone else to do, blocks the manifestation of your own dreams. So, return the library books, the hammer, the videotape, the cordless drill, and anything else that someone lent to you in good faith. Use the item, take care of the item, and return the item. Do not hold on to things that do not belong to you.

Integrity goes the extra mile. It is returning the neighbor's car with a full tank of gas. It is wiping down the cordless drill you borrowed from your friend. It is washing down the mower before it is returned.

## HOW WILL YOU KNOW IF YOU ARE
## NOT IN YOUR INTEGRITY?

Read the signs that are generously provided along the way. You will notice that things are not going as easily or as smoothly as they once did. For instance, you get a large, unexpected car repair bill, or the water heater breaks. Of course, these things do happen. However, when such unexpected experiences are consistently dropping their bags on your doorstep, it may be worth looking at your integrity.

A lack of integrity drains the positive flow of good from your life. Life will be more of a struggle than an ease. Recently I spoke with a woman who could not understand why her life consisted of so many unusual day-to-day struggles. She told me of the many financial strains in her life, and how the furnace in her home broke, the pipes froze, and her car kept stalling. "It has been one thing after another," she told me. I invited her to review the violations of integrity. She did not realize that the incomplete projects in her life were disrupting the flow of good into her life. She had been avoiding opening her mail, as she was overwhelmed with overdue bills. The bank was considering foreclosure on her home. She had been abandoning so much of her life, and subsequently, life was becoming increasingly burdensome.

Take an inventory of things in your life that have not gone the way you had hoped or intended. Perhaps business has been poor, or you have had the flu or a cold. Perhaps you are waiting for money that has yet to arrive, your son is doing poorly in school, you did not get into the college course you wanted to take, or your mother forgot your birthday. When such unexpected events happen in your life, choose to find the lesson hidden within. There is something that you need to know or change. Life is our teacher, and it is up to us to be an attentive student. Be willing to listen and to learn.

The Integrity Checklist (see appendix) is a valuable tool for getting honest with yourself and with others. It is not meant to overwhelm you or to discourage you. It is simply a tool to aid you in identifying your personal issues of integrity. There may be things on the list that you do not perceive as integrity. That is okay too. Integrity is often historically and culturally defined. Therefore, different people will have different interpretations of integrity. Your definition is the right one for you. Simply check off the things that fit with your definition of personal integrity.

It may seem like an endless task to stay in your integrity. However, like anything that seems trying at first, it tends to get easier with time. Be mindful. There will always be opportunities for you to step out of your integrity. It is not always easy to do what is right. At times you will be tempted by what seems easier or more convenient. Good integrity is an ongoing process. Integrity is demonstrated through your daily decisions and actions.

Integrity lives in the light of day for all to see. It means that anyone at any given time could peek into your life, and you will feel at ease. There is nothing to hide and nothing to be ashamed of. You are simply living your life with integrity.

# Chapter 7

# The Language of Abundance

Fear less, hope more, eat less, chew more; whine less,
breathe more; talk less, say more; hate less, love more;
and all good things are yours.

--Swedish Proverb

Words communicate your needs and desires. Therefore, the spoken
word is essential to manifesting your dreams. The problem arises in that
you often say what you do not mean. You may not realize the impact of
your words.

That is just the way it goes.
I do not have the money.
Just watch, he will not do it.
It is just my (bad) luck.
It is not going to make any difference.
I will never make it on time.

I have done that. It does not work.
I doubt it.
I will never be able to get the time off.
I knew that would happen.

*Words often communicate your fears rather than your desires.*

Common language communicates lack and contradicts your desires. You automatically communicate your fears about things that you do not want to have happen. Take for example the common term "I can't afford ..." You tell other people that you cannot do certain things because you cannot afford to do them. You speak of living in lack and scarcity.

*God is listening. What are you saying?*

Your Higher Power is listening and is eager to deliver your desires. Words are your spoken intentions, and yet you typically use words that imply lack and limitation. For example, consider the use of the word budget. You say, "I have to stay in my budget," or, "It's not in my budget." The purpose of a budget is to have enough money to pay your bills and still have a little extra cash at the end of the month. Yet the word budget implies lack and limitation. It communicates that there is a limit to your finances. It means that you just can't "budge it." It's a dead end. A budget indicates that your finances are fixed and unmovable. It implies that you cannot go beyond a certain amount; there is "not enough." Due to its feeling of deprivation, some people respond negatively to the idea of maintaining a budget. They are afraid of being deprived of their needs and desires. Often people avoid creating and maintaining a budget as they associate it with restriction and limitation. Yet those that honor a budget often have money left over at the end of a month.

Common vocabulary often echoes pessimistic thoughts. It seems natural to focus on the negative rather than the positive. You speak negatively with little forethought. You ask others, "What is wrong?" and, "What's the problem?" in everyday communications.

Negative words exacerbate your fears and cause unnecessary misery. Negative talk causes feelings of frustration, fear, and worry, which only lead to premature failure. "I'm not going to make it," implies that you have already failed. A person has not failed until all the scores are settled.

*You fail first in your mind, and then in your affairs.*

Self-defeat begins in your thoughts. For instance, you believe that you will be late to a meeting. Subsequently, your words are "I'm going to be late." The Universe observes that your thoughts and words are consistent, and therefore begins to assist you in accomplishing that which it believes you desire. And so, you get in your car and realize that you have forgotten your keys. You quickly race back into the house to retrieve your keys. To make up for "lost time" you drive as fast as possible. Suddenly, the traffic ahead of you stops due to a construction delay. "I'm going to be late," you tell yourself anxiously. Finally, you move beyond the construction only to find that you are further delayed by numerous traffic lights. The lights seem longer than usual. By this time, you are feeling distraught and in a state of fury. You hastily park your car and start running toward the building. You are late. The meeting has already begun. In a hurry, you suddenly realize that you have forgotten your briefcase in the back seat of the car. You race back to your car. The clock keeps ticking. You finally enter the meeting out of breath and out of sorts. You apologize profusely to those people affected by your tardiness and blame the delay on the long lights or the construction. However, the truth is that you received exactly what you asked for. The Universe was listening.

*Speak of what you want to have happen rather than what you are afraid will happen.*

When was the last time that you could not find something that you needed? You misplaced a receipt for something that is broken and needs to be returned to the store. You search the house in a panic while repeatedly saying to yourself, "Someone threw it away! It was here yesterday and now it is gone. I just know it was thrown away!" Are you really hoping that someone threw away this receipt that you now need? Of course not. So why are you telling the Universe that this is what you want to have happen? Your negative words only increase the likelihood of not finding the receipt. It is what you are asking to have happen. Your chances of finding the receipt are just as good if you declared, "It is here. I know it is here. I will find it." You will also feel better.

Eliminate words that oppose your desires. Speak only of what you want to experience. Avoid statements that include the words not, can't, don't, won't, and never. These words contaminate phrases and speak of failure rather than success.

Take out a piece of paper and make a list of your common phrases. Notice those phrases that speak of defeat and failure. Take the time now to find alternative phrases that speak of success. For example, instead of saying, "It won't happen," simply state, "It will happen." Replace the phrase "I can't afford that now" with "I choose not to spend my money on that at this time." Choose words that speak only of success.

Develop a new and different language that communicates abundance rather than limitation. Although budgets serve an important purpose, they do not have to imply limitation. Instead of a budget, choose to create a "financial success plan." It is like a budget in that it gives a general picture of personal finances. It tracks income and expenses. Yet a financial success plan expresses abundance rather than lack. Wouldn't you prefer a financial success plan rather than a budget? Learn to speak positively about all the things in your life.

*Quit your complaining.*

Complaining is an avenue through which we use our negative words, and although it is commonplace in our society, it is destructive to the art of manifestation. Complaining blocks, the flow of prosperity. When you speak negatively of people, places, and things, you obstruct the flow of good into your life.

Although it is natural to complain, there seem to be people who are more experienced at complaining than others. Complaining is a hobby for some people. Yet the truth is that we all know how to complain. We complain about our work, our numerous household chores, our financial affairs, and our family members and colleagues.

It is as if the act of complaining serves a purpose in life. Complaining can alleviate boredom. If you feel bored, you might complain, as it gives you something to do. Complaining invites attention or sympathy from others. It also serves as a way of socializing with other people. People like to commiserate with others. "Misery loves company." We like to have an audience. What would be the point of complaining if nobody were around to hear the complaint?

The interesting thing about complaining is that we rarely complain about our own actions. Instead, we complain about others. We complain when we feel unjustly treated, and we complain about prices and fees for services or products. We "haggle" with salespeople in hopes of getting a lower price. We convince ourselves that this is an effective way of managing our money. It is not. It is not up to us to determine the fees of another. It is, however, our option to choose to utilize or not utilize such services, or to purchase or not purchase the item. You can certainly decide whether an item is something that you want, but you are not in your integrity to choose the price.

Sometimes you may complain to get someone else to assume responsibility for an inappropriate action or reaction. I refer to it as the "you made me do it" phenomenon. It does not matter what happened, it only matters that you made me do it. This is something that stems from childhood when you felt it necessary to blame a sibling or peer. You assign blame: "It's his fault, not mine."

> The Johnson teenagers were horsing around at a family reunion picnic site. They were having a fun time throwing water balloons and smearing shaving cream on one another. It was great fun. However, while throwing water balloons at one another, a glass panel of a window was shattered. When the park official came to assess the damage, he simply stated that it was "okay" and that there would be a nominal charge to replace the panel. Rebecca, one of the teenagers, reacted with anger and hostility. She angrily told the

official that he had no right to charge them and complained of how slippery the steps to the pavilion were and how she could have slipped and been hurt.

It is easy to find things to complain about. You complain about your bills and about how much you must pay in taxes to the government. You complain about your job and about the weather.

Complaining comes from an internal place of discontent and unhappiness. To complain is to demonstrate to others how unhappy and dissatisfied you are with yourself and your life. It exposes your misery. Complaining also attracts more things to complain about.

There is no benefit to complaining about your life. Consider what it would feel like to live without whatever it is you are complaining about for a specific time. For example, say that you are complaining about your car. You do not like all the money you have had to put into repairing it lately. What would it feel like to leave your car home for just one day? You could take public transportation instead or ask your neighbor to drive you to work. Imagine what your life would be like without your car. Sure, you would not have to complain about it or put money into it, but would your life be simpler? If you are complaining about the cost of your electricity, choose to go without lights for a few nights. You will quickly realize how you take privileges for granted. Learn to celebrate what you already have instead of complaining about what you do not have.

Complaining repels good from your life. If you complain, you defy the laws of prosperity and abundance, which include trusting that your needs are always met.

*Stop anticipating struggle.*

Nick, a salesperson at a car dealership, was in the process of completing the necessary paperwork for selling a car, which would earn him a commission. He needed to telephone the auto insurance carrier to arrange coverage for the customer. As he began to dial the telephone, Nick told the customer that "this insurance company is difficult to work with. There is never anyone there to talk to."

Nick had already established his negative beliefs and was anticipating struggle, so how could the process be anything but difficult? His chosen words spoke of complication, and his emotions of frustration and resentment ensued. Negative thoughts and words generate a negative outcome. It is a simple equation.

Negative + Negative = Negative
Thoughts    Words    Outcomes

In addition to complaining, you may also share hardship stories. You tell others that you are at risk of losing your job, that the car repair bill is outrageous, and that you are having a "bad day." You are more willing to recount the "trials and tribulations" of your life than the victories and successes. Why do you do that to yourself and others? Perhaps you hope to gain the sympathy of others. Or you want others to recognize how well you cope with struggle and strife. Regardless of the reasons, to talk of hardship attracts more hardship.

*Share success stories rather than hardship stories.*

You may use words that relate catastrophe or defeat. Everyone feels defeated and hopeless on occasion. Everyone entertains thoughts and ideas that are negative and destructive. Surrender your hardship stories. Leave that for the newspapers. Instead, share your success stories. Talk of the good that is happening in your life. In doing so, you are inviting the good in your life to multiply.

As you learn the language of abundance, you can teach others as well. You can teach others to reframe their negative thoughts and words into something more constructive. To reframe is to take your thoughts and words and transform them into something that is more useful, productive, and, of course, positive. Reframe. It is merely a change in words.

I met a woman who frequently said, "Life is a struggle." I encouraged her to replace the phrase "a struggle" with the word good. By simply changing a word, she created a positive and affirming statement—life is good. Examine for yourself what a significant difference a slight change can make. Reframing another's words can be so powerful. The unfortunate part is that although others appreciate such encouraging words, they may remain doubtful that the words will make any difference in the actual outcome. But just maybe the experience gave them a little something to think about. It is fun to affirm good things for people even when they are affirming negative experiences. Positive talk eventually catches on—it is contagious.

As you speak positively of the things in your life, you attract positive things. Once, while on vacation, I was determined to get a free t-shirt from the resort, which was selling t-shirts with the company logo on them. I told my friend, "I am going to manifest a free t-shirt." A few days later, my friend and I were sitting in a quiet space, relaxing, and enjoying the scenery. There were numerous beverage glasses that had been left behind by others, and we decided to return them to the appropriate area. As we walked down the path to return the glasses, we saw the exact t-shirt that I had asked for days earlier, laying on the ground before us. It was brand new. It was the desired color and size. We both looked around in amazement to see if anyone had mistakenly dropped it. There was no one around. I paused and gratefully thanked God for yet another wonderful gift.

Your words have the power to generate your fortune. When you put your positive words together in clear, authoritative statements, you create affirmations. Affirmations set your intentions. Therefore, they are necessary in the process of manifesting your dreams and desires. Affirmations are the simplest way of creating the most wonderful and enriching life experiences. They are positive expressions of what it is you want to experience in your life. Affirmations communicate your genuine desires and bring your dreams into fruition.

*Affirmations must clearly represent your intentions and desires.*

Affirmations cannot be vague or ambiguous, lest they produce confusing and undesirable results. They must be clear and concise in meaning. Be clear about what you want to have and to experience in life. Affirmations are spoken with authority. Mean what you say.

Affirmations must be stated in positive and encouraging words. They are stated and written in the present tense, as if they are already occurring. This allows you to make a clear statement of what you want to have happen. Affirmations communicate your belief in the manifestation of your desires.

> Marjorie wanted to vacuum her car at the local car wash. The sign read that the vacuum only took quarters and required five quarters to start the vacuum. Marjorie grabbed her wallet, and realized she only had four quarters. She refused to entertain the idea that she would not be able to vacuum her car. She looked in various places in the vehicle. She checked under the seats. She repeatedly told herself that she would find just what she needed to get the car vacuumed. After a few minutes of searching everywhere possible, she was unable to find an additional quarter. However, she did find a dime. She viewed it as if the Universe were giving her a dime instead of a quarter. She decided to try the dime in the machine, and it began to work. She proceeded to vacuum her car and graciously thanked the Universe.

*Affirmations speak only of success.*

The following are examples of affirmations:

- I am financially secure.
- I am in excellent health.
- I have all that I need.
- I am confident.
- All my needs are met.
- I am worthy of all good.
- The Universe knows what is best for me.
- I live in abundance.
- I am happy with the good that life continuously offers
- I attract only good into my life.

The *Dynamic Laws of Prosperity* is a valuable resource for affirmations. However, it is essential to create your own affirmations as well, as needs and desires are personal. As you develop your own affirmations, write them down (see appendix). In that way, you can easily refer to them until they become familiar.

As summer was changing into fall, Catherine realized that her daughter had quickly outgrown her warm clothing. Rather than panicking, she simply told herself, "What is needed is already on its way." Later that same day, she went to a friend's home for a visit. During the visit, the friend (unaware of her need) asked her if she would like clothes that her children had now outgrown. Catherine could not believe it. She went home with three shopping bags full of warm clothes for her daughter.

*Goals put words into action.*

Although words are powerful in manifesting dreams, it is not always enough to simply verbalize your goals and dreams. Words must be followed up with action. Goals are the written expression of your desires. They are affirmations in a written form. By writing down your goals, you invite them to manifest into your life.

There are many people who struggle with setting goals. They find it difficult to think of goals and are ineffective in accomplishing them. Similarly, there are people afraid that their goals will not be met, and therefore avoid setting them. They are afraid of feeling disappointed or, worse yet, they are afraid of failing.

Goals give direction. They are the maps that lead you toward the destination of your dreams. You need goals. You need goals for the day, the year, the next six months, the next year, and the next five years. Without goals, it is easy to lose your way. Goals keep you moving forward.

Goals are the specific steps of action that allow you to manifest your dreams. They make the impossible possible. For example, imagine that you want to go back to college. The process begins by simply writing down this goal on a piece of paper. To simply keep a goal in your mind is not sufficient. They must be written down. This is the first action that is taken toward its manifestation.

*Goals must be written down.*

Write down your goals on a regular basis. It is a simple strategy; so simple in fact that this is the reason many people have not implemented such a powerful plan-—it seems too simple to work.

Once you have written down your goals, you can proceed in developing the steps that put them into action. For each goal, ask yourself the question, "What will it take to get me there?" If an answer does not come forth, close your eyes to gain the help of your inner wisdom. The answers to this question serve as the actions needed to achieve this goal. The specific goals for the example of going back to college include (1) research the Internet for schools in a certain area or that offer your field of interest; (2) narrow this list down to three possibilities; (3) call for more information and request necessary forms and applications; (4) review information; (5) decide; and (6) enroll.

> For years, Maria talked about going to college. The fact that she was a woman in her forties with two children and an unsupportive husband painted a grim picture for her dream to manifest. She worked for an insurance company while she continued to dream of getting a college degree. Due to feelings of discontent, she decided to participate in the Women's Support Network, offered through my practice. The group teaches women to establish and meet their chosen goals. The group gave her the encouragement and enthusiasm to follow her dreams. She decided to "try" a college course the following academic semester. Four years later, she sent a card announcing her graduation.

Goals enable you to move toward success. Take the time to write down your personal goals (see the goal sheet in the appendix). Include a completion date for each goal. Track the progress of your goals by checking off goals as they are met and setting new goals as needed.

-When the New Year arrives, create goals instead of making resolutions. Resolutions tend to be temporary and self-defeating. Goals, on the other hand, have a better reputation. The word goal may evoke the response, "Wow, good for you," while the word resolution may evoke the response, "Yeah right, we will see." Goals have a reputation for being accomplished, while resolutions have a reputation for being dismissed. Therefore, create a New Year's ritual of setting or revising your goals. Goals keep life moving in the direction of your dreams.

Goals must be always visible. Avoid hiding them in drawers or storing them in your wallet. Instead, post your goals on a bathroom mirror or a spot where you can see them on a consistent basis. Visibility is important in enabling your dreams to come true. Allow them to be visible to you and to the Universe.

Protect your goals and dreams. Be aware that there will always be people who will challenge your goals or shame you for having them. Goals are personal, and therefore only belong to you. No one else must like them or approve of them. The only criterion for them to be met is that you believe they can happen and are committed to making them happen.

As a child growing up on Long Island, I dreamed of living in the mountains. I would tell my parents that "someday I am going to live in the mountains." As is the case with most parents, they responded with, "Okay, we'll see," and rarely gave it a second thought. As time moved on, my goals became more specific. I shared with my parents my desire to go to college. Again, I received a similar response. My senior year arrived, as did the time for applying to colleges. My parents were unaware of the strength of my desire to go away to college. Their idea of success for their children was to be "gainfully employed" as soon as possible, to work hard, to earn a good wage, and to someday retire with a good pension. Although my parents were delighted with my decision to attend college, they assumed that I would attend the local two-year college. I was the first of their children to consider attending college. However, I held strong to my desire to live in the mountains, so I only applied to colleges that were in the mountains. Much to my parent's surprise, I was accepted to the college of my choice, which was six hours away from home. They were supportive, but shocked.

*All things are possible when you put*
*your mind and effort into it.*

Goals have been and continue to be an integral part of my life. Many dreams have manifested through the straightforward process of writing down goals on a sheet of paper. In fact, all the wonderful things that I have acquired thus far in my life were once written down on paper—a graduate degree, a private counseling practice, a beautiful log home with a mountain view, two healthy children, a laptop computer, various vacations, and several vehicles, including a conversion van. However, my goals were frequently met with a great deal of sarcasm and disbelief from others. Credibility only comes after you make things happen for yourself.

*Goals are not accomplished overnight.*

Goals take time. They rarely materialize overnight. Therefore, the actual manifestation of your dreams requires patience. Without patience, you are at risk for abandoning your dreams prematurely. The formation of goals is like the planting of seeds in a garden. A garden requires consistent care and cultivation before the harvest. Pay close attention to your goals, to prevent them from withering and dying. Remain diligent as your dreams are worth the effort and the wait.

*Goals must be reasonable.*

Your dreams can be extraordinary. It is not necessary to limit your dreams. However, your goals toward accomplishing your dreams must be reasonable and attainable. Goals must feel within your reach, otherwise you will surrender to feelings of frustration, discouragement, and defeat.

Goals can include the telephone calls that need to be made, the information you need to obtain, or the resume you need to update. As time goes on and you are consistently accomplishing your goals, then you are ready to "up the ante." It is then that you can set more challenging goals. By that time, you have developed a variety of tools that work to accomplish your dreams, and you are not as vulnerable to the feelings of discouragement and defeat. Then, dream big! Dream in color!

Believe in your dreams and desires. Believe that what you want, or need will happen.

> For several years, Grace kept a piece of paper that contained a list of book titles that she wanted to eventually purchase for her office. One day a client of hers brought in a large box of books that she no longer wanted. The client thought that Grace might be interested in the books. As Grace went through the box, she was surprised to find several books that had been on her list.

It is amazing how easily the things you need manifest when you simply ask. Recently I needed a fish tank for the new fish my daughter was inheriting from her first-grade classroom. I decided to go to a local consignment shop to see if they had one. They did not. I asked an employee if fish tanks were ever brought in for sale. She stated that she had occasionally seen them in the store. She took my telephone number and told me that she would call me if someone brought in a fish tank. The next day I received the call. Your needs, too, are always met.


AND JUST A WORD ABOUT WORK . . .


Work is the primary means with which you derive an income to support your lifestyle. Yet people have a great deal of negative things to say about work. Many people are unhappy with their chosen job or career. They resent their work or the mere fact that they must work. They were taught to merely "work for a living." Thus, they have learned that the sole purpose of work is to put food on the table and gas in the car. Have you, too, been taught that work means doing a grueling job that gives you no joy for the sake of a paycheck? Unfortunately, that is what most people settle for regarding their work. They do not see beyond the need for a paycheck.

When you work for a living, you tend to sacrifice the emotional ideals of being happy or excited about what you do. Although you may desire to be happy with your job, this is not perceived as a necessity. The paycheck is what is necessary; happiness is the rare bonus.

*Your work is your primary source of prosperity.*

Where you work is how you make your money. Therefore, if you view your work in a negative manner, you block the flow of money into your life. Be mindful of the actual words you use to describe your job, your bosses, and your work environment. Negative thoughts and words have the potential to make matters worse. Negative words cause you to dread each Monday morning as you begin a new workweek.

*Enjoy your work while earning a good salary.*

Your work is significant to who you are and what you desire in life. You are on this earth for a distinctive reason. There is work for you to do here. The problem is that most people do not know what that work is, and therefore are not doing it. It is common to settle for "working for a living" rather than spending the time and energy needed to discover your "life work." Your life work is the type of work that your Creator intended for you. Life work is easily recognized by the feelings it invokes. It is work that you feel the most passionate about. It is work that offers excitement and enthusiasm. It is work that you cannot wait to start doing and cannot imagine having to stop.

Your head may tell you that it is not possible to "earn a living" doing something that you love. You have learned that love and work do not fit together. Therefore, you think that you must wait until retirement to do what you love. "When I retire, I am going to open my own cafe." You think you must wait to meet your needs and will not allow yourself to do something now when you want to do it. Take the risk necessary to put love and work together. The truth is that the more you like your work, the more income potential there is for you.

Mike worked at a plant for several years to provide for his family. He lacked the self-confidence needed to pursue what he really wanted to do, which was bodywork on cars. He did not trust that his skills were "good enough" to receive pay for something he enjoyed. Therefore, he chose to work on people's cars at a significantly reduced rate or as a favor to gain the experience, as well as the confidence. As his self-worth and self-confidence improved, he was able to accept a position doing just what he enjoyed. He is now getting paid for what he loves to do and released the job he had to do for a living.

Life has so much to offer. Remember, life is not intended for you to struggle. And if you are merely working for a paycheck, you are struggling. There are no joys found there, just blood, sweat, and tears. This is not the case for everyone, however. If you love what you do and are paid well for what you do, move on to the next chapter. If not, stay right here.

People need to be willing to embrace work that is fulfilling and rewarding. Yet there are many reasons for staying in jobs that are unrewarding. For instance, if you feel unworthy of having a "good" job or a rewarding career, you are not likely to pursue the job or career. Like Mike, you perceive yourself in an undesirable light, and give yourself only what you think you deserve. Perhaps you think that you lack the ability to do what would enhance your life. This represents those negative and debilitating feelings of shame and inadequacy. You believe that you are incapable, so you choose work that is laborious and burdensome.

People remain in unhappy jobs when they feel "stuck" or "trapped." They have been at the company for a long time and do not think that it will be possible to work anywhere else. They convince themselves that they do not know how to do anything else. Their salary has grown to a point that it does not seem likely that another employer could match it. They are afraid of losing that which they have already acquired. They believe that there will be more to lose than to gain.

People are afraid of taking less money, especially if they are already "struggling to make ends meet." There is not a great deal of flexibility when a person is "living from paycheck to paycheck." These are just two of the negative phrases that are commonly used.

> Dawn is a single parent who worked at a local university to pay her bills and provide for her two children. She took the job because of needing an increased income following a divorce. The job, however, was stressful and unrewarding. Dawn found herself crying a great deal, particularly when she had to leave her children each day to earn a paycheck. Through the therapy process, she was encouraged to look at what her job was doing to her emotionally as well as what it was doing to her relationship with her children. Prior to this job, Dawn had owned a day care business, which she enjoyed. However, the day care did not pay enough to meet her increased financial needs. After careful consideration, Dawn made the decision to leave the university job. She chose to take a summer off and spend it with her children. She affirmed that the right job would come in the fall. In late August, she was hired as a teacher's aide in her local school district. Dawn again loves what she is doing. She has what she needs: work that is fulfilling, and time with her children.

*Prosperity comes from doing what you love.*

Although it can sometimes feel as if there is no conceivable way out of an unhappy and unfulfilling job, there are ways. Those ways may not seem visible to you. Instead, your thoughts keep you imprisoned in a job or career that you do not like.

When you maintain thoughts of struggle, you live with struggle. Therefore, you work more hours during the week "just to keep your head above water." Consequently, your work hours steadily increase while your quality family time steadily decreases. You sacrifice family and leisure times in pursuit of prosperity that rarely seems within your reach. Prosperity is rarely accomplished in this way. And if it does somehow find its way to you, there is good chance that you are too busy to enjoy it. In this way, you are working for prosperity rather than letting prosperity work for you. True prosperity comes when your heart is full. In the world of work, that means doing only what you love to do.

Prosperity requires risk. You must be willing to move past your fears and take the necessary risks to grow, to change, and to prosper. Of course, I am not telling you to quit your job. I am only telling you to keep your eyes open for the opportunities that may come your way. Recognize opportunities. Be willing to listen and to try them on whenever possible or appropriate.

You are given many opportunities to grow and to prosper. Do not pass them by on your quest for something else or by accepting the "path of least resistance." If opportunity knocks, at least open the door.

EXERCISE

On a scale of 1-10, assign a number that rates how happy you are in your work life at the present time. Let one represent feeling miserable and unhappy (you would leave tomorrow if given the opportunity) and let ten represent feeling incredibly happy and satisfied in your job (you have no desire to change it in any way). If you assigned a number that is less than 4, you really need to rethink your current work situation.

You must be happy in your work. After all, that is where you spend most of your time. When you choose work for the mere paycheck rather than for the joy or challenge, you are choosing struggle. Work is not meant to be something you agonize over. Work in a job that you enjoy. If it is not possible to leave your job at the present time, explore ways to make your job more pleasant or challenging. Create a work atmosphere that you love. Describe your work, your coworkers, and your environment in positive ways. Decorate your space, no matter how small, with pictures and words that inspire you and remind you to enjoy the life that you have. Display pictures of your family or your pets. Make sure that there is sufficient lighting. Make it pleasant. Make it truly a space that you enjoy working in.

Apply for promotions or other positions that are of interest but apply only if they are truly of interest to you, and not based on a change in salary or position. Make decisions regarding a job based on what you will be doing for eight or ten hours a day. Is it something you would love to do or would love to learn how to do? Will it be rewarding or challenging? Decide what is important to you regarding your job.

Do you desire a lavish office, a prominent title, or flexible work hours? Remember that prosperity knows no limits. Let yourself fantasize about what it is you would genuinely love to do. If you could do one thing for forty or more hours per week and be amazed that you are being paid to do it, what would you be doing? If you could create the ideal job, what would it include? Write down your responses.

Embrace work as the good thing that it is. Choose only work that you desire. You make the choice to work where you work and do what you do. Learn to love what you do or choose to do something different. Take the risk to be happy and to be prosperous. Stop waiting. Live with ease rather than struggle.

And I tell you, ask and you shall receive,
seek and you will find:
Knock and the door will be opened to you.
For everyone who asks, receives; and the one who seeks, finds;
and to the one who knocks, the door will be opened.

—Luke 11: 9-10

Ellen Peterson

Chapter 8

# Prosperity Through Pictures

Dreams begin in the mind. Build through the word.
And materialize with visualization.


Can you picture yourself living in the home of your dreams? Can you see yourself walking across the stage in a cap and gown? In other words, are you able to see your dreams coming true? You now know that your words can move a dream into reality. "A picture is worth a thousand words." Visualization allows you to see and experience your dreams coming true prior to their actual arrival in a physical form.

*Visualization uses the mind to*
*produce desires.*


Imagination is an essential element of visualization. Your imagination enables you to picture something that is not yet visible to the human eye. Therefore, visualization may be simple for some people, while challenging to others. The ability to visualize comes naturally to some people. They can see the result in their imagination, or minds-eye. This ability is a gift, as those who are unable to do so will surely attest to. How well are you able to visualize things in your mind? Are you able to see things before they exist in a physical form? Can you see what the living room will look like before you rearrange the furniture? Can you picture a new home, yourself in a particular career, your checking account with a specific balance? Are you able to imagine the things that you would like to have or experience in your life? Can you see these things? If the answer is yes, then you will find visualizing your dreams to be quite simple. It may be as easy as closing your eyes and seeing yourself seated in a college classroom or behind the wheel of a fancy new vehicle. For others, it is not so simple.

> Carol's car was in the repair shop on a regular basis. It was costing her significant amounts of money to maintain this car that she no longer wanted. She longed to replace it with a dependable, yet inexpensive, car. When asked to close her eyes and visualize such a vehicle, she strongly stated, "I don't see anything." Instead, she was distracted by her thoughts of how she would pay for a new vehicle. These thoughts prevented her from the joy of seeing herself in a new car.

Everyone is born with an imagination. However, your ability to effectively use your imagination may have been thwarted in the obstacle course of life. Imagination is developed through childhood play. Therefore, if you were discouraged from being imaginative or playful, these natural abilities may have been affected, suspended, or entirely thwarted. The imagination also tends to fade over time with increasing age. Adulthood inhibits playfulness and a lack of imagination inhibits visualization. Therefore, you close your eyes only to see nothing, and feel quite inadequate and frustrated. You quickly abandon your dreams when you are unable to see them. When life throws you its challenges, you lose hope and surrender. You jump overboard at the first sign that there may be trouble up ahead. You forget that you can simply steer the boat in a different direction.

The imagination is not visible, so it is easy to convince yourself that what lies in the imagination is not real or possible. However, your thoughts are also not visible, yet so easily believed. When you deny yourself the use of your imagination, you are restricted to believing only the visible, the tangible, and the concrete. This places you at a disadvantage because so much in life is not visible and tangible. Faith, trust, and inner wisdom are not usually found in a physical form. Do not limit yourself to the tangible things you can see with your eyes. Supplement your physical eyes with the eyes of your mind.

Strengthen your ability to imagine and to visualize. Close your eyes on occasion and stimulate the wisdom that dwells within you. The other senses become more acute to compensate for the loss of vision. Develop and use your imagination. Learn to see, believe, and trust in the invisible as easily as you do in the visible.

EXERCISE

Close your eyes for a few minutes. Take in a few deep breaths, taking the breath all the way down to the soles of your feet. Focus only on the breath as you take it in and bring it down. Breathe in and breathe out. Now, imagine yourself on a beautiful beach. You are alone and just quietly resting on the white sand. Feel the warmth of the sun on your face. Feel the sand on your skin. Hear the waves of the ocean as they crash onto the shore. Listen to the seagulls in the distance. Be aware of the familiar sounds in this place. Notice how relaxed you are here. Let yourself stay in this relaxing place for as long as you like, and then open your eyes to the present space you are in.

Visualization is a valuable tool for inducing relaxation. Visualization gives fantasy a reality. You can feel as if you are in that imagined place, even while sitting in the living room of your home or at the desk in your office. Guided imagery has been proven effective in the treatment of stress and anxiety. It offers the mind and the body some "downtime" that is typically not provided otherwise.

Guided imagery has been proven effective in the treatment of stress and anxiety. It offers the mind and the body some "downtime" that is typically not provided otherwise.

Visualization is enhanced by the senses. Therefore, sharpen your senses and improve your ability to visualize your dreams. Begin to use your senses fully. Look around you and take note of what you see, hear, feel, and smell. Experience life through your senses. The experience of touching and smelling a rose is much greater than simply seeing a rose.

Awaken your senses to experience the fullness of your imagination. It will serve you well in life. Use your mind to its fullest potential. Do not keep it idle and asleep. Use it to create and enrich your life. The mind helps you to visualize your desires, prior to the manifestation of your dreams. Visualization allows you to see the possibilities.

Kerry had purchased a raffle ticket with the hope of winning a door prize. She was interested in one prize: a newly released CD of her favorite rock band. As she held her raffle ticket in her hand, she closed her eyes and imagined herself winning the prize. In her visualization, Kerry heard the announcer list the item, and then her name, Kerry Martin. She visualized herself excitedly pushing her way through the crowd, and clearly saw her facial expression as the man placed the CD into her right hand. She heard herself saying, "Thank you," and saw herself turning away with the CD in her hand. Kerry completed the visualization and opened her eyes to the sight of more people gathering around the person who would be announcing the winners. She affirmed, "I am now the proud winner of the CD," and repeated this affirmation to herself repeatedly. Gradually, she was becoming more solid in her belief that she was going to win that CD. All doubt and fear of disappointment was fading. By the time the announcer began the raffle, she was certain that she was going to win the CD. Now, she just waited to collect her prize. She stood patiently and applauded other winners of assorted items. When it was time to give the CD away, she closed her eyes and reviewed her visualization. Just then, the announcer held up the CD that she had already seen herself winning. He shook up the raffle tickets once again and drew a name. "Kerry Martin," he nonchalantly announced. She had won the CD with the help of her imagination.

Pictures are essential to those who are unable to visualize their dreams and desires. Pictures compensate for what you are unable to see with the mind's eye and give life and realism to your imagination. Your dreams, which begin in the imagination, must be developed into concrete pictures.

Pictures hold a value for most people. Whether they hang on walls or are prominently displayed in frames, they are nice to have and nice to share with others. You take pictures while on vacation to remember the experience. You treasure photos of your loved ones. You order yearly school pictures. You take more than one picture of the same thing, "just in case the first one does not come out well." Pictures stimulate your memory, provide enjoyment, and enhance your life. Pictures make you smile.

There has been an ongoing evolution of the photography industry. There was a time when people relied on cameras with film and a flash. The film had to be developed at which time you would know how the pictures turned out. The digital age has since allowed for viewing photos immediately upon taking them. Most people currently rely more on their cell phones to take photos then on a camera, thus eliminating the need to carry a camera in addition to a phone. Selfies, or photos taken of oneself, have become increasingly popular. Regardless of how pictures have been and continue to be taken, pictures are indeed important.

Bill and Susan lived in a beautiful home. One day, in the early morning, they suddenly awoke to the startling sounds of the downstairs fire alarm. They quickly and safely evacuated their home. From the neighbor's yard, they watched as the fire destroyed all that they had owned. As weeks and months passed, they were able to rebuild their home and replace the furniture and other material possessions. Their greatest loss, however, was their wedding photographs and pictures of family and friends. They were, in fact, irreplaceable.

Time does "march on." Pictures of times now past are not so easily replaced. Time passes and we are left with our memories and whatever pictures were taken at that time. In this way, pictures increase in sentimental value with time.

Pictures may be kept in wallets, photo albums, on our desks, and on our refrigerators, and they remind us of those we hold dear and who mean the most to us. Photos provide us with a sense of connection during the times we are not physically together. Pictures are special and enhance our daily lives. They have the potential to brighten our day. Therefore, it may not be surprising to learn that pictures aid in the manifesting of your dreams.

Catherine Ponder refers to this ancient prosperity law as the Law of Imaging. It is the ability to visualize the actual image of what it is you would like to attract into your life. It is the ability to see your dreams before they come true. This is accomplished either by your mind's eye or your physical eyes.

*Pictures help to manifest your dreams.*

Your dreams begin with a thought. Thoughts are invisible, and because they cannot be seen with the human eye, they provide you with something concrete to look at while your dreams develop in the invisible. Pictures give your dreams reality before the dreams appear in your life in the physical form.

> Lisa and Barry dreamed of a new boat. They wanted to replace their current boat with a larger one to accommodate their growing family. As they looked through a boat magazine, they discovered a picture of a boat that they loved and desired. They cut out the picture and put it on their refrigerator, where it could easily be viewed. It served to remind them of their dream. The picture remained on their refrigerator for several months. As others inquired about the picture,

they told them that it was a picture of their next boat. Within the year, they proudly owned their new boat. Pictures allow you to imagine your dreams coming true, so you need to use them effectively to manifest your dreams. Actual pictures of your dreams and desires are instrumental in the manifestation of their reality, so create a visual representation of your personal dreams and desires. It is truly fun to do. It is much like creating that Christmas wish list as a child.


MASTERPIECE TO RICHES

A Masterpiece to Riches is a simple and effective tool to use for manifesting your dreams and desires. To get started, take a poster board, and cut out a circle. The circle represents continuity and acknowledges your spiritual connection as your source of unlimited supply. Glue pictures or words in the center of the circle that acknowledge your spiritual connection. For example, you might include words such as "God is in the Details," or pictures of angels, a cross, a flower or other representation of your Divine Source. Continue to cut out various pictures or words from magazines and newspapers that best represent your dreams and desires. Search for pictures of that dream car, new computer, fresh look, or vacation destination.

It may take time to gather the most suitable pictures and words. Think about the kinds of things that you may want to include in your Masterpiece to Riches. Search magazines in your home and office. Download and print desired images. Temporarily store your selected pictures in an envelope while you continue to search and collect others. Once you have enough pictures and words, you are ready to create your Masterpiece to Riches. Do not be concerned if you do not have all the pictures of your dreams, as it will be possible to add more later.

Do not clutter your pictures, as you might do on a collage. These are not merely pictures, but pictures of your dreams and desires. Therefore, do not lay one over another. They need to be displayed in a clear and obvious manner. They must be visible to you at a glance. Make your personal Masterpiece to Riches bright, bold, and colorful to reflect your interest, enthusiasm, and excitement. These are your dreams.

As you know, pictures are simple to find and to clip out. Therefore, the Masterpiece to Riches is a simple project. The problem is that it requires time and energy. Be willing to invest the time and energy to manifest your dreams and desires.

*It takes time and energy to make dreams a reality.*

Do not allow skepticism to stand in the way of making your dreams a reality. It is unfortunate when people get stuck in the belief that such a project will require a great deal of effort and energy. They feel overwhelmed by the mere thought that it will be a lot of work, so they never begin creating their Masterpiece to Riches. Their thoughts once again prevent their dreams from moving into reality.

> Betty first heard about the Masterpiece to Riches in a group therapy setting. She liked the idea and immediately began to collect pictures of her dreams and desires. At the age of forty-five, she wanted to own a business, something she had always wanted to do. She included a picture of a professional woman on her Masterpiece. She cut out the face of the stranger and replaced it with a picture of her own face. Within a couple of weeks, she was reporting to the group that she had begun researching the need for her business in the community. Betty was the only person in the group who had chosen to create a Masterpiece to Riches.

The others did not think it would really make that big of a difference. It certainly did. Now, three years since creating that initial Masterpiece to Riches, Betty is the proud owner of a successful small business.

Many people are reluctant to believe that something so simple could bring their dreams into fruition. They think, *how will a mere picture of a new vehicle manifest the real thing?* The honest response is, "It will." As stated earlier, we need to reprogram our thinking from that of struggle to that of ease. The only requirement is that you create a Masterpiece to Riches. It is not how you do it that matters, it is only that you do it. Do not allow perfectionism to stand in the way of manifesting your dreams and desires. Once it is complete, you will be amazed at how quickly and easily your dreams begin to manifest in your life. It is amazing!

> Eileen owned a small number of shares of Walt Disney stock and wanted to increase the number of shares. As she created her Masterpiece to Riches, she included the words "Disney Stock" on her colorful poster board. She would walk by that poster board several times a day and notice those obvious black words. A few months later, she received a notice that the stock had split. She now owns twice as many shares of Disney stock.

Dreams manifest with little effort when you can see them in a physical form. However, you need to update your Masterpiece to Riches so that it always reflects your current desires. As time goes on, you will notice that a great deal of the images and words on your Masterpiece to Riches have already manifested. Be prepared to update your masterpiece every one to two years. Simply transfer the pictures and words of those things that are still in the invisible onto a new poster board. Add new pictures and words that represent your current desires.

*Keep your Masterpiece to Riches current*
*with your dreams and desires.*

Recognize and accept, however, that although you can place your intentions into the Universe by using words and images, you are not in the position to determine the outcome. You do not determine when, how, or in what way you receive your desired gifts. That is, of course, up to the giver. You need to simply trust that your desires will manifest at the right time. Remember, trust is the foundation of prosperity and abundance. In addition, you must always set your intentions in a clear and concise manner. Do not waiver in doubt or mistrust.

Doreen wanted to promote her business in the field of Creative Arts. She spent months creating brochures and flyers advertising theater camps for children. She had set an intention to have 130 students registered for the summer camp. She visualized this repeatedly in her head each day. Only a few weeks prior to the start of the camp, she was offered a job working for a school in New' York City. She decided to take the job and relocate to alleviate financial burdens. She hired others to teach the camp. She did not get the 130 children for the camp. She came up short in her goal and struggled to understand why. She made her intention and used visualization every day.

What went wrong in the process of manifesting this desire? The answer is simple: Doreen switched her focus to something else. Through her action, she changed her intention. She had unknowingly confused her message to the Universe.

*Pay attention to the details.*

The process of manifesting your dreams and desires requires an "attention to detail." It requires you to be mindful of your spoken words, your actions, and your visualizations. Be mindful regarding the pictures and words that you place on your poster board. Assemble with caution, as "what you see is what you (may) get." As you create your Masterpiece to Riches, be mindful of the pictures you choose and the way in which you arrange them onto the poster. Place on your poster only what you truly desire and not something that "will do for now." Do not waste time, space, or energy on anything that is less than your true desires. Ask for what you want; do not settle for what you think you can have.

As is true with your spoken word, your pictures must be consistent with your actual desires. Do not confuse the Universe by having your pictures reveal one thing and your thoughts and words reveal something completely different. They must be consistent; otherwise, there will be a disruption or delay in the realization of your dreams.

> Lee had wanted a gold, two-tone Lexus SUV, so she searched for a picture of a Lexus and placed it on her Masterpiece to Riches. After a year, she could not understand why the vehicle had yet to manifest. She reported consistent use of the various tools of manifestation, and yet there was a delay or block to her desired good. When discussing her chosen picture, she stated that it was a picture of a blue Lexus SUV, as that was the only picture she could find. She was informed of the discrepancy between what she wanted and what she was presenting to the Universe. She was unable to find a picture of a gold Lexus, so she decided to write the word "gold" across the blue vehicle on her Masterpiece to Riches. The gold Lexus SUV manifested only six weeks later.

It is amazing to see your desires come to fruition with the use of imagery. To glance at your own Masterpiece to Riches and recognize the things that have already manifested in your life is powerful. It seems as if they manifest with little effort. However, if things manifest in an unexpected way, you may want to review your spoken words, or the pictures displayed on your Masterpiece.

> Anne had wanted a house on the lake. She found and placed a picture of a lake on her Masterpiece to Riches. Some months later she was looking carefully at that same picture. She realized that although she had not yet manifested a lake house, the mountain view in the background of the picture had been remarkably familiar. She recognized the view as being like that of her most recent vacation destination. Although she did not manifest a house on the lake, she manifested a wonderful vacation to a majestic place such as the one in the picture.

As with your goals, your Masterpiece to Riches must also be kept visible. It is best to view it in the morning as you begin your day, and then again at the very end of your day. If it is displayed in a noticeable area, it is likely that you will be viewing it on a regular basis. Visibility aids in the manifestation of your dreams and goals.

> Donna had created a wonderful Masterpiece to Riches. She was creative in the pictures that she chose and had organized them in a systematic way. However, she became frustrated that her dreams were not manifesting in the anticipated time. As she reviewed the obstacles that prevent or delay prosperity, she could not find any reason for such a block in the manifestation of her dreams.

When I asked her where she kept her Masterpiece to Riches, she casually stated, "Under my bed."

*Dreams must always be visible.*

Hiding your dreams implies that you are either ashamed of them or you doubt that they will ever come true. Believe in your dreams; know that they will come true. Display your dreams and desires and guide them toward manifestation.

There are alternatives, but still effective, ways of creating a Masterpiece to Riches. For instance, if you work a great deal on a computer either at work or at home, it may be fun to create your Masterpiece to Riches as a screensaver. Scan some pictures of your desires and create a screensaver that comes on when the computer sits idle for a period. Use your creativity to discover the best way for you to display your dreams. Perhaps you prefer to hang individual pictures of your dreams on your refrigerator or on your bathroom mirror. The important thing is that they are visible.

My own Masterpiece to Riches is displayed on a cork board in my bedroom. I awake to it each morning and glance at it again as I retire each night. It is bright, bold, and colorful. It is a consistent reminder of where I am headed on this road in life, and what I am looking to accomplish. It motivates me. It allows me to stay clear and focused on my personal goals and dreams.

*Allow pictures to do the work for you.*

After you have invested the time needed to create your personal Masterpiece to Riches, just sit back and watch what manifests. It is amazing. Best of all, it is that simple.

Chapter 9

# Gratitude: The Heart of Prosperity

*If the only prayer you say is thank you, that will be enough.*

Meister Eckhart

Gratitude is the heart of prosperity. In the same way that the heart serves a vital function in the human body, gratitude serves a vital function in prosperity and abundance. Gratitude is the way in which you acknowledge the good that exists in your life. Life offers greater beauty and color when you are filled with gratitude. It is an expression of appreciation. "Thank you" is the most used phrase in our culture to express gratitude. This phrase is used to acknowledge and appreciate someone or something. Although they are two simple words, they have a tremendous effect on your attitude, as well as on your life experiences.

People can forget to acknowledge the good in their lives. They approach life with feelings of defeat and frustration rather than with confidence and gratitude. They often look beyond the good that they have in search of more. They believe that "there has to be something more." These familiar feelings of "not enough" create cravings for more. Many people are on a perpetual search for more—more time, more money, and more stuff.

In this quest for more, they lose sight of what they have and how far they have already come. Most people are now too busy to "stop and smell the roses" on their path to fulfillment. They are in hot pursuit of finding something more, or even something else. They view life as if it were a huge mountain to climb, with an even larger one right behind it, and therefore there is no victory or celebration once they have climbed to the top of the mountain. Instead, they see what still needs to be climbed.

Gratitude is part of the celebration. It allows you to pause and to see what you have accomplished or what has happened in your life. It allows you to appreciate life, and to stop and absorb the good that already exists in your life.

*God is the source of all good.*

Gratitude is a way in which you acknowledge the good in your life. It acknowledges the handiwork of God. When you believe that there is no such thing as coincidence and that there are no accidents, you accept the gift of grace. Grace is the channel through which we receive Gods intended good. Therefore, gratitude becomes an automatic response to recognizing God's grace. Grace does not ensure that you will not suffer, but that you will never suffer alone. God offers grace in the face of tragedy and trying circumstances. The many good things that already exist in your life come from your Creator. Grace is a divine gift, and divine gifts are not to be overlooked, taken for granted, or returned. The good in your life is a true blessing from above. When good things happen in your life, acknowledge the Divine Giver with a simple "thank you." It is polite to acknowledge the gift, as well as the Giver.

Although God is continually sending good your way, you may withhold your gratitude until something extraordinary happens, such as a loved one surviving a difficult surgery. You may be grateful for the bigger favors and thoughtlessly ignore the many smaller favors. You may choose to be grateful only after you receive your desires. In this way, you perceive prosperity to come before gratitude. That is, you receive and then you feel grateful. There are many wonderful things that bless your life each day. Be thankful for the extraordinary *and* the simple blessings.

Gratitude is more than being thankful; it is a positive view of life, a certain set of glasses through which you see and experience the good in life. Gratitude brings into focus what is going right rather than what is going wrong. Gratitude magnifies the good and preempts negative emotions. You are less likely to feel frustrated and irritated when you feel grateful. Gratitude guides you to feel differently about your circumstances, your life, and yourself.

*Gratitude is the key to attracting good into your life.*

There is a holiday devoted to giving thanks. Thanksgiving brings families and friends together to be thankful and to appreciate the good in your life. Learn to recognize and appreciate the good in your life throughout the year. Look around you. Notice the many things surrounding you that make your life comfortable and enjoyable. Appreciate the simple things in your life. The chair you are sitting on is a gift. Your voice is a gift. Your hot cup of coffee is a gift. Each moment of your life is a gift. Recognize all that is good.

Personal health is the greatest of gifts. Health is a significant part of prosperity. My mother often teaches, "When you have your health, you have everything." Many people take their good health for granted, but following the gift of life, health is your greatest gift. The fact that you exist in this life is, of course, your primary gift. Without life, there is nothing else. In a comparable way, without good health, it is difficult to enjoy life. It is more challenging to get through a typical workday with something as common as a headache or a cold. The slightest adverse change in your health affects your performance. It causes you to move at a slower pace. Even simple tasks are much more difficult to accomplish. People who are in good health tend to find other things to worry and complain about while those in poor health worry about nothing else. Good health should not be taken for granted.

> Josh is a thirty-three-year-old young man who had been considered popular and "perfect" in high school. He was voted class president. He had a supportive family and a bright future. He eventually went on to have a beautiful family of his own and a promising career. Life was good. But one day his life suddenly veered off course. While skiing on vacation with his family, he had a tragic accident that left him with a traumatic brain injury. Life as he knew it changed dramatically.

The status of Josh's health changed quickly and dramatically. The quality of your life can change at any given moment. That is a sad but notable truth. Life indeed changes with any change in your physical health. Be grateful and acknowledge your good health.

*Rely on foresight rather than hindsight.*

Appreciate each moment. The secret to embracing life is to simply live in the present, not in the past and certainly not in the future. The truth is, you may grieve for the past and feel anxious about the future. You long to return to the past because it is familiar. You can spend a great deal of energy and time trying to recreate the past, as good or bad as it may have been to you. Additionally, you worry about what lies ahead. You fear the future rather than look forward to it. The future is a complete unknown to everyone. Through life's experiences, you were taught to fear the unknown. It is not possible to be fully in the present when you are worried about the future. Then, as the future moves into your present, you momentarily feel relieved and then quickly return to worrying about what will happen next.

When things are going well, you "wait for the other shoe to drop." Learn to accept things as they are. Live in today. Be present in today, in this moment. The rest will take care of itself because God is in control.

Close your eyes for a moment and be present to yourself. Go within. Be still. Be quiet. Be reverent. This is truly the only moment that matters. Feel the moment. Take this time to feel something that surrounds you, a blanket, or the fabric on the chair. Develop the ability to be in a moment. In doing so, you are not likely to miss it when it passes. In living in the moment, you are also less likely to have regrets. Regrets only occur when you look back into the past and convince yourself that you have missed something. Now that the moment is gone, you wish you could go back and do things differently.

You are more likely to feel grateful when you are living in the present. A perfect example of this is during a family vacation. Many people anticipate the end of the vacation and begin to grieve while still on vacation. They may still have two wonderful days on the beach, but instead they are saddened by the fact that the vacation will eventually end. This is truly a waste of wonderful "lifetime." Our time in this life is to be enjoyed and savored. Every moment counts.

*Live in the present, instead of in regret.*

Gratitude is a wonderful teacher as it enables you to be more aware of life. Gratitude diminishes fear and welcomes joy into your life. It regenerates your love for life.

PRACTICING GRATITUDE

Appreciate the many people who bless your daily life your spouse, your children, your parents, your siblings, your friends, and your neighbors. Imagine for a moment what your life would be like without their presence. Yet it may be easier to be kinder to strangers than you are to your own family. Although you may feel frustrated with others at times, you will always long for the love, support, and companionship that come from your relationships. Therefore, let others know that you appreciate their kind words, gestures, or actions. Be generous with your praise and words of appreciation. Let others know that you value their presence in your life.

Take the time today to express appreciation to at least two members of your family. Say thank you. Tell them that you love them. Tell them that they are important to you. Praise their efforts. Put a note in their lunch. Offer them a hug. Call them during your workday. Do something nice for them. Verbalize and demonstrate your appreciation for others. Show appreciation to your coworkers and colleagues as well. Tell them how much you value their wisdom, insight, knowledge, or sense of humor. In doing so, you develop stronger and healthier relationships, and you open the channel of abundance.

> Jack and Linda have been married for ten years and have two children. They were both aware of the increased distance in their relationship. They no longer had much to say to each other. When they did talk, it became an argument in which both blamed the other for the problems in their relationship. Consequently, they found themselves avoiding one another. Neither one felt valued or appreciated by the other. Instead, they felt taken for granted. They began to feel unloved and disconnected from each other.

This is a sad but familiar story. Couples detach and disconnect emotionally from one another when they no longer feel valued or appreciated. When these niceties of a relationship are absent, the relationship deteriorates. The feelings of hurt and resentment develop.

Many couples long for how they treated each other when they first met and dated. In truth, they are longing for the attention and appreciation, which is typically present in the initial stages of a relationship. If you did not receive consistent praise in your childhood years, you may continue to look for it in your adult relationships.

*Replace criticism with appreciation.*

Appreciation is the life raft for marriages. Most marriages dissolve today not because of abuse, but because of a lack of attention and appreciation. You get so caught up in the day-to-day routine of life that you neglect your significant relationships. Consequently, you gradually lose sight of what is important. You lose your ability to listen attentively and to be compassionate. It is easier to describe yourself as a loving and compassionate person than it is to behave in a loving and compassionate manner. Thus, you tell your spouse that you love him or her as you continually criticize how he or she loads the dishwasher or folds the laundry.

When you feel upset and angry, you are not compassionate and loving. Be compassionate and loving when it is not the easiest thing to do. Relationships thrive on compassion and kindness. Begin today to appreciate, validate, and encourage another family member. Put it on your daily to-do list. Be understanding of the feelings of another. Avoid condemning and criticizing others. Offer an ear and simply listen. It is all anyone truly needs.

*Gratitude renders kindness.*

Nourish your intimate relationships. Take the time to periodically write down specific things that you are grateful for in your spouse or partner. Does he or she take out the garbage on occasion, iron your shirts, or schedule your doctors' appointments? Does he or she make sure your car inspection is current, or your lunch is made? Recognize that there is usually a mutual exchange of acts of kindness.

Invest in your relationship. A fire will not burn forever without attention and an occasional stoking. Stoke the fire of your relationship. Give it the time and attention that is necessary for it to continue to thrive. Relationships are a key factor of the good life. Express your gratitude to those who share your life.

Greet each day with a grateful heart. Acknowledge the many things that you are already grateful for today:

- An alarm to awaken you.
- Time for breakfast
- A hot cup of coffee
- Your bed
- Your children
- Your pets

- Gas in the car
- A refreshing shower
- Heat and electricity
- Time with family
- A paycheck
- Your health

Your life consists of an infinite number of gifts, many of which you have not even realized. It is a gift to see a sunset. It is a gift to have a job to go to each day. It is a gift to see the smile of a child and to hear laughter. Recognize and appreciate life's many gifts.

Make a list of the things that you are grateful for today (see appendix). A list such as this shifts your focus from the negative to the positive; from what is wrong to what is right. It allows you to bring the focus and energy to the things that really matter in life.

*What you focus on multiples.*

Sarah Ban Breathnach, author of Simple Abundance introduced the "gratitude journal." It consists of using a journal or notebook to write down a minimum of five things that you are grateful for daily. A gratitude journal highlights the positive experiences of your life. It enables you to reframe your thoughts and feelings from negative, nonproductive thoughts to positive thoughts and prosperous feelings. It is a simple yet structured way to say "thank you" for the gifts in your life. It may be challenging at first to identify things to write in your gratitude journal. Begin slowly. Write down anything positive that comes to you. It can be as simple as having hot water for your shower in the morning. The important thing is that you write something down. Developing a grateful heart is a process. It takes time. As time goes on, it gets easier. You will find yourself saying throughout a day, "I have to remember to write this in my gratitude journal."

*Gratitude restores balance and*
*opens the channel for prosperity.*

The gratitude list is a powerful tool to use when things are veering off the prosperity course. When your furnace breaks, your plane is delayed, you cannot find your birth certificate, or you encounter another unexpected occurrence, it is time to sit down and make a list of things for which you are grateful. When such unfortunate things happen, a simple gratitude list can make the necessary shift from negative to positive. It changes the focus. It changes consciousness. When the flow becomes blocked, gratitude serves as the liquid plumber.

> Margaret was presenting at a conference. Just prior to her presentation, things were going wrong. She discovered a rip in her pantyhose. The slide projector would not work, and she could not locate the custodian who could fix the projector. She was becoming increasingly anxious when she remembered the benefit of writing down a gratitude list. She quickly reached for a pen and paper and took a few minutes to write down the things that she was thankful for that day and in her life. She found herself more relaxed and confident, and decided that she could present her material even if the projector were not working. People were slow in arriving, so she went to the hotel store and purchased a new pair of pantyhose. As she introduced herself to the audience, the custodian walked in to look at the projector. Just as she was ready to use the projector, the custodian announced to her that it was fixed. It all worked out well, and now she had even more to be grateful for.

All is well when you are grateful. Keeping a daily gratitude journal is an effective way to reopen the prosperity channel and keep it clear and flowing abundantly. When things are going astray, do not despair. Simply sit down and write all the things for which you are currently grateful to have in your life. It is a quick fix, and it will get your life back on course.

The gratitude list is only one of many ways that you can express gratitude. You can also express gratitude through words and simple gestures. For example, you can do something nice for someone else as a way of expressing appreciation. Our culture has specific customs that encourage the expression of gratitude. For instance, tipping is a way in which you express gratitude to those who provide a service for you. Employers may give year-end bonuses to recognize the work of their employees. You give gifts to the teachers of your children. You send thank-you cards. You know that it is right to express gratitude. However, there are times when you convince yourself that your actions are sufficient in demonstrating your gratitude and appreciation. For instance, you may think, "Well I make his lunch every day, so he knows how much I appreciate him." However, your actions must supplement your words, not replace them. Learn to become equally adept at using both forms of expression of gratitude: doing and saying. Develop effective and consistent ways of expressing your gratitude to others and to the Universe for its never-ending gifts to you.

*Claim your good*

It is unfortunate how much good passes through our lives without our awareness. Small gifts are easily overlooked and often go unnoticed. To be prosperous, you must not only pay attention to the good, but you must also claim the good as yours. Your good belongs to you. Surrender the belief that good things only happen to other people. Good things happen to you, too.

Take for example the last time you noticed a penny on the ground. What did you choose to do about it? Did you ignore it and simply walk past it, pretending it was not there? Did you pick it up and put it in your pocket? People respond in diverse ways to this common situation. Those who choose to walk past the coin may do so for fear of being judged by another. They do not want others to think that they need a mere penny. Then there are others who choose to pick it up in a swift manner. They also fear being judged by others, or they just want to get it before someone else does. Then there are some people who simply pick up the penny with the belief that it is a gift of prosperity from the

Universe. Reflect for a moment on your own thoughts and reactions when seeing money on the ground.

Pennies, like any other money used in our culture, need to be equally respected and acknowledged. Pennies were once thought of as tokens of good luck. They are tests in prosperity. Can you appreciate and value a penny? Or do you experience it as invaluable and meaningless?

> Today I found a penny, just lying on the ground.
> But it is not just a penny, this little coin I've found.
> Found pennies come from heaven, that is what my
> grandma used to tell me.
> Grandma said, Angels always toss them down.
> Oh, how I loved that story.
> She said when an Angel misses you, they toss a penny
> down
> Sometimes just to cheer you up, and to make a smile
> out of your frown.
> So don't just pass by that penny when you're feeling blue.
> It may be a penny from heaven, that an Angel's tossed
> to you.
>
> —Author Unknown

There are people who throw pennies in the garbage, as they consider pennies worthless. If pennies were truly worthless, they would be extinct. Yet they continue to exist, and we continue to make use of them. Many stores now have little dishes in which they keep pennies for times when a customer is a penny short or needs a penny to receive more convenient change. Pennies are good; they serve a valuable purpose. As a young child, I spent many hours helping my father sort and count pennies. It was through this experience that I came to appreciate and value the penny.

Learn to acknowledge and accept all good that comes your way. Enjoy the arrival of prosperity, no matter how it comes or in what denomination. Simply say, "Thank you."

> Jean wanted new furniture for her living room. She had
> seen the ideal sofa and chairs at a local store during its

winter clearance sale. The price was right. However, she already had a high credit card balance and did not want to incur additional debt. She wrote daily in her gratitude journal, accounting for the many blessings in her life, including having found this furniture. She decided to inquire about financing options through the store. She learned that they had interest-free financing for one year. It enabled her to get the furniture she desired without increasing her credit card balance.

*Embrace all gifts with gratitude.*

Embrace the good in your life. Feel worthy to receive. Allow others to help you and to do things for you. Receive your good. When was the last time a person asked if he or she could help you? You were carrying numerous things, and someone asked if he or she could help you carry something. Were you willing to receive help? Or did you resist a kind gesture by saying, "No, thank you. I am okay. I think I can manage." Although it may feel awkward and unfamiliar, learn to receive. The next time someone volunteers to help you, simply respond with, "Yes, thank you." Even if you do not need the help, say, "Yes." Let someone do something nice for you, and experience how wonderful it feels and how simple your life becomes. Let someone hold the door for you or carry your grocery bag to the car. Stop struggling. Learn to receive instead.

Nancy felt uncomfortable when others paid her a compliment. She used humor to deflect or minimize the compliment. When a colleague told her how nice she looked, she responded, "Oh, you have not seen me in a long time. I have gained a lot of weight."

Allow others to compliment you without tossing the compliment back at them. When someone pays you a compliment, simply respond with "Thank you." Avoid making excuses or justifying why something is so. Avoid criticizing yourself or critiquing the compliment. Surrender that ugly feeling of unworthiness, which prevents you from receiving what we all need—to feel worthy, valuable, and important. Become accustomed to the simple response of "Thank you." It is not necessary to say anything more. In time, you will grow comfortable receiving compliments from others, and may eventually come to believe them, too.

Many people feel uncomfortable receiving material gifts from others. They feel embarrassed, and may inadvertently push the gift away, saying, "Oh, you shouldn't have," or, "I wish you wouldn't do things like this." These responses reflect a person's insecurities and inadequacies. They reiterate those feelings of unworthiness and indicate that a person does not feel deserving of the generosity of others. Accept the kindness of others. Receive compliments, gifts, and kind gestures with gratitude. In doing so, you will pave your way to greater prosperity.

Gratitude opens the channels of prosperity. However, you must cultivate and maintain a place of genuine gratitude within yourself. Prosperity is dependent upon living in gratitude, not visiting it once a year. Gratitude allows you to feel rewarded and "blessed," which causes you to react favorably to the people and things in your world. Gratitude brings contentment and fulfillment.

As you incorporate gratitude into your daily life, you create a vacuum through which greater good can come. You know and believe at a deep level that your good, whatever that may be, is on its way. With a grateful heart, you spend less, complain less, and have more. You know and appreciate what you already have; there is little else you need. Be grateful.

Gratitude is the way in which you give thanks to the Universe, your source of supply. Therefore, gratitude is a key factor in enjoying permanent prosperity, as it keeps you in the flow of prosperity. It enables you to embrace the good in life. All that is needed is a simple "Thank you." Enjoy your good with gratitude.

# Chapter 10

# Giving: The Gateway to Manifesting Dreams

You cannot hit the jackpot if you don't put in a coin.

--Flip Wilson

Giving is a part of the system of exchange. St. Francis of Assisi asserts, "For it is by giving that one receives." Therefore, it is necessary to "put in" in order to "get out." You must deposit money before you can withdraw it. There must be an investment before there can be a return.

Giving is the gateway through which you manifest your dreams and desires. Imagine for a moment having a gate in front of your home. As the gate opens and swings outward toward others, it creates an opening through which good can come back to you. As you give generously to others, you open the channel of good to you.

Breathing is a natural illustration of the concept of giving and receiving. Each breath consists of an inhale and an exhale. The exhale represents giving, while the inhale represents receiving. It is difficult to inhale without the exhale. This is also true in the process of manifesting your desires. It is difficult to receive without the occasional giving.

Although everyone possesses the same potential for being generous and giving, some people give more freely than others. Take this opportunity to explore your feelings about giving to others.

How do you feel when you give to others?

When do you give?

To whom do you give?

Why do you give?

How much do you give?

Do you give freely, or do you give reluctantly?

Feelings vary about giving. Some people enjoy giving, while others resent it. There are many reasons for giving. You may give to impress. You may give to delight. You may give to appreciate. You may give to apologize. You may give to be liked or respected. You may give to be recognized or acknowledged. People who give consistently are considered generous. They may be perceived favorably as "noble," "kind," and "good." Most people would rather give than risk being perceived as "selfish," "greedy," or "stingy." You want others to think highly of you, so you give. Sometimes you give because you want to, but too often you give because you feel obligated to give. You give because it is someone's birthday. You give because it is Christmas. You give because he is "my father." You give to avoid hurting another person's feelings.

Kate was shopping for a Mother's Day card. She knew that she had to send one to her mother or risk being given the dreaded silent treatment for months. She searched for just the right card. Kate's relationship with her mother had always been strained, and she struggled to find a simple yet kind card. She could not bear the idea of telling her mother how great she was and how loving and supportive she had been throughout her life. That was not her personal experience. She finally settled on one card that simply read Happy Mother's Day.

Some people struggle when choosing a card for someone with whom they do not have a close relationship. They may not have had the endearing relationship that cards typically honor. They give because they feel that they are supposed to give.

The Christmas season is a specific time of year when you are expected to give to others. It is known as the "season for giving." It is also considered to be the most stressful and expensive time of year. This is the reason many people are miserable during the holidays. Most people give themselves a mere month to prepare for the holiday, only to become overwhelmed by the lengthy and never-ending to-do list. People resemble millions of mice on the treadmill vying for the same cheese. The rushed feeling of time running out leads to feelings of frustration, craziness, and exhaustion. Is it any wonder that many people dread the season rather than enjoy it?

Christmas is the season for feeling pressured to find the perfect gifts for those you love. You want them to like what you give them, which may steal from the enjoyment of giving. You may find yourself waiting in lines and dealing with tired, frustrated cashiers to please someone else. The holiday season has become one unpleasant chore after another, yet year after year you do the same thing despite your promises that "next year will be different." You vow to buy less, shop less, or decorate less in hopes of experiencing more joy in the season. Then you quickly lose sight of your needs and panic because you have many things to do in a brief period.

You feel resentful when you are pressured to give, yet you are constantly bombarded with solicitations for money and donations. Solicitations come by telephone, mail, friends, family, and coworkers. "Please give." "We need you to give." "We need your help." "Give generously." "We rely on your generous donations." You give charitable donations to organizations that serve others. You give to the SPCA, the Red Cross, the American Cancer Society, and various other noble organizations. You give to the police and the fire departments. You give to the church and to the food banks. You drop off clothes and other items at the Salvation Army. You purchase candy and magazines to support schools and organizations. You buy Girl Scout cookies. You support your alma mater. There are countless opportunities to give throughout the year. The truth is that most organizations and businesses would not survive without the monetary support of others. There will always be people asking for money because there will always be people who need money.

Although this type of giving is important, it is not the type of giving that invites good things into your life. Feeling obligated or forced to give rarely produces feelings of kindness and generosity. Obligatory giving will not manifest your desires. When you give out of obligation, you are not giving from the heart. You are choosing to give because of feeling "trapped" or "backed into a corner." The flow of good and abundance is blocked and trapped as well. Yes, you have given, but the truth is that you did not actually want to give.

*Conditional giving inhibits abundance.*

Conditional giving is commonplace in this society. Most people expect something in return, even if it is just an acknowledgment. You do something for someone else in hopes that they will return the favor. Although you may say that you do not need anything in return, you often feel hurt or resentful if you give and do not get something back. You want to receive a "thank you." You justify your need for something in return. "It would be nice to know that they received it." It is not that you want to act in such a way. You have been conditioned by previous generations to expect something back.

You play the notorious "Giving Game." It consists of two players, one responsible for giving, and one responsible for receiving. The giver carefully watches the receiver's every move. A camera may even record this important moment. Will there be a favorable reaction? Will the gift be appreciated? Will the receiver like it? Will the receiver perceive the giver as generous? This can be a fun game to play if the receiver is aware of the rules. If, for instance, the receiver responds negatively, then both parties lose.

This game also includes "giving because of having been given to" cards. Each card represents something that has been given to you, that you must remember to give back later. For example, make sure that you send a birthday card to someone who was nice enough to send you a card on your birthday. If a present was given, make sure that you give something of equal value. This may indeed affect what you had wanted to give, as it does not cost the same, but it is not worth losing the game. Another important rule in this game is "don't give to one without giving to the other." If in doubt, give to all.

Also, make sure that you feel horrible and ashamed if the other person gives to you and you have nothing to give in return. You must give while trying to avoid receiving. Good luck.

There is only one true reason to give—
because you want to give.

Learn how to give unconditionally to others. Give because you want to, and not because you must. Give with love and without any expectation of getting something in return. Give from the heart. There is no acceptable dollar amount when giving from the heart. Unconditional giving means giving without an equal exchange. It is an act of love and genuine kindness. It is simply giving.

There are as many ways of giving to others as there are reasons for giving. It is most common to give something of material value, such as clothing or jewelry. You shop the malls and department stores looking for something that might please someone you care about. Photographs and baked goods are also lovely and thoughtful gifts. Money is a universal gift often given to acknowledge a special occasion, such as a graduation or retirement. Money is given as a way of saying, "Congratulations," "Thank you," "Happy birthday," or "Thinking of you." It is given when you are unaware of what someone may need or desire. Money is a gift that is appreciated by all, and it is also quite easy to send, as there are no bulky packages to wrap or special postage needed. In addition, money is not returned for improper fit or wrong color.

Generosity does not always accompany a price tag. It is possible to be generous to others without the monetary expense. For instance, you can give generously of your time by volunteering your services to others. You can bake for the bake sale, count money for the church, and sing in the choir. You can volunteer at the library or the animal shelter. You can serve pizza at the local school, deliver meals to the homebound, or visit patients in hospitals and nursing homes. Volunteers are the backbone of many communities. Your time is valuable; it is a gift that you give to yourself and to others.

Time is essential when it comes to nurturing your relationships with your friends and family. They need your time as well. Too often, people attempt to compensate for their lack of time by giving material things, yet most people would gladly surrender the material things for more time with a loved one. Therefore, it is important to recognize that giving your time is just as important as giving money or material items.

Giving takes many forms, from the simple to the extraordinary. Consider the many simple things that you can give to others.

A smile

A hug

A word of encouragement

A call to say hello

Holding another's hand (touch)

A thank you

A helping hand

Kind words

A card

Kind gestures

These are small yet significant ways to give to others. They require little money, and a small amount of effort. They are simple enough to give daily. They offer warmth and a tenderness that material gifts rarely offer. These gifts are more typically remembered. They are simple ways of giving something extraordinary to someone else. So, bring your spouse a cup of coffee, pick up your kids from school on occasion, bring home flowers, volunteer to make breakfast on a Saturday morning.

Kristen had just moved into a new apartment in a small town. As she was unpacking some of the many boxes, there was a knock at the door. She could not imagine who could be at the door, as she was so new to the community. She cautiously opened the door and saw a young woman with a plate of brownies. The woman simply stated, "Welcome to our neighborhood. I am Maggie and I live in the blue house across the way. I brought you some brownies to enjoy while you are unpacking. I also thought you would like some important telephone numbers of organizations and businesses in our community." Kristen was deeply touched by such a genuinely kind gesture. She holds its memory forever in her heart.

When you give, you are typically giving to others. This is, of course, the most common definition of giving. In fact, many people find it easier to give to others than to give to themselves. But you need to be able to give to yourself as well. Take responsibility for meeting your own needs while giving generously to others.

Many books on how to achieve financial success recommend giving to yourself before giving to others. You are encouraged to "pay yourself first." Yet you are programmed to give to others first and to "wait to see if anything is left over" for yourself. This not only refers to finances, but to physical and emotional energy as well. You put yourself last on the list. You get the crumbs if there happen to be any left. This eventually leads to feelings of anger and resentment. You feel cheated.

Learn to give to yourself as easily as you give to others. There are many simple ways in which you can be kind and generous to yourself. Sit down and enjoy your morning coffee rather than taking it on the road with you. Read a few pages of an uplifting or inspiring book.

Telephone an old friend. Take a walk. Play with your pets. Take a warm bath tonight or a nap on a Sunday afternoon. Be willing to pause in your day and in your life. Take time out to relax, reflect, or simply breathe deeply. Delegate some of your responsibilities to someone else. Do something that you have been putting off for a long time. Read in bed. Watch the sunrise. Take an excursion to the mall alone. Take some needed time for yourself. Replenish. In giving to yourself, you fill your personal well with water. When your own well is full it is that much easier to give to others.

Extend your giving to the Universe. The Universe is the giver of all gifts; it deserves to be recognized, too. It is easy to convince yourself that if you are giving to others, you are indirectly giving to the Universe. This may be true. However, is it enough? If you had to pay someone for every wonderful blessing in your life, how much would that cost? You are fortunate in that the Universe does not ask for compensation to that degree; the IRS is a different story. However, it is necessary to support the continuation of spiritual teaching and practices. Be willing to give to that person or place that provides you with spiritual growth and fulfillment. By doing so, you contribute to its ongoing ability to meet your spiritual needs. It is not possible for churches, ministries, and social service agencies to survive without money. They also have expenses, which can only be paid for with cash. Catherine Ponder clearly reminds us of the fact that "God needs cash."

> Dare a man rob God? Yet you are robbing me!
> And you say, "How do we rob you?"
> In tithes and in offerings!
> You are indeed accursed, for you, the whole nation,
> rob me.
> Bring the whole tithe into the storehouse,
> That there may be food in my house, and try me in this,
> says the Lord of hosts:
> Shall I not open for you the floodgates of heaven,
> To pour down blessing upon you without measure?

Malachi 3:8-10

Take care of your churches and your ministries. It is mutual nourishment. You take care of them, and they take care of you. Take care of all that you need to survive and thrive, including your spirituality.

Tithing brings prosperity and abundance. Tithing is discussed many times in the Bible (Genesis 14:20, Genesis 28:22, Leviticus 27:30, Numbers 18:26, and Deuteronomy 14:22-29), yet some spiritual and religious organizations emphasize tithing as a spiritual practice, while others do not.

*Tithing is essential in manifesting prosperity.*

Tithing is accepted to mean giving 10 percent of one's income or revenue to a church or spiritual organization. The number ten is depicted in the Bible as "the magical number of increase." Tithing is giving to one's place of worship, such as a church or synagogue. It is a gift of gratitude and appreciation. It keeps the lights and the heat on. It ensures that there will always be a place or a person that nourishes you spiritually. Tithing provides a structure that allows for consistency and fair giving to the Universe and takes into consideration what you have and what is possible to give.

Many people resist the practice of tithing. Some resent being told that they must give a certain amount of their income to their church or religious organization. Some people feel that they do not have the money to give and fear that they will not have enough money to meet their own needs. They further question why it is necessary to give to a church or organization when "no one gives to them." Resistance is noticeable when you play with the percentages. For instance, people question whether they should tithe from the net income or gross income. Should they give what feels comfortable or what does not feel comfortable? Tithing consists of giving 10 percent, which still leaves you with the other 90 percent.

> Give plenty of what is given to you, and listen to
> pity's call;
> Don't think the little you give is great, and the much
> you get is small.
>
> —Phoebe Carey

Many books on prosperity will tell you that the best time to tithe is when you feel that you have nothing to tithe. During such times, choose to tithe the small amount that you do have.

*Tithing is a gift of gratitude.*

There have been times when Joanne tithed and times when she has chosen not to tithe. "When I tithe, I notice that the money is there not only for tithing, but for my monthly expenses as well. However, when I have not tithed because I did not think I could, I struggled with not having enough."

Giving creates a vacuum for receiving. What you give or how much you give is for you to decide. Keep in mind that what you give will eventually be returned to you, so give with some thought. If you give money, it is money that will be returned. If you give time, time will be returned. If you give material things, material things will be returned to you. Decide what you want to have, and then give generously and consciously.

Fear tells you to give what you can or what you have available. You believe that if you had it to give, then you would give. Your feelings of scarcity provide you with a convenient excuse for not giving. Yet you always have *something* you can give. Your life is full of material things that sit idle in closets and on shelves. As you release the things that no longer serve a purpose for you, you also surrender the fear of not having what you need.

Surrender the needless time and energy you spend worrying that your needs will not be met. If you review past times in your life, you will see that your Higher Power did indeed get you through the lean times. The mortgage got paid, the children got sneakers, and your husband got a new job. God has and always will take care of you. Reflect on how God has provided for you thus far in your life. The truth is that God gives to you every day. God is most certainly the greatest of Givers.

The important thing is to give as much as you can
—That is what God accepts,
And no one is asked to give what he has not got.

—II Corinthians 8:12

Recall the classic story "The Gift of the Magi." The story is about a man and a woman who love each other but are without gifts to exchange. Without telling each other, both decide to trade their most treasured possessions to purchase something for the other. It is a story that truly represents the concept of giving from the heart. The story ends with him selling his watch to buy a barrette for her beautiful, long hair, which she sold to buy him a chain for his watch. They gave each other the rare gift of unconditional love. Would you be able to give away your most treasured possession, even to someone you love?

As you realize that your needs are always met, you can give freely and generously. Fear no longer holds you back. Furthermore, the knowledge that your needs are met enables you to gratefully receive from others.

> Please accept my gift that is brought to you, because God has dealt graciously with me, and because I have everything I want.
>
> Genesis 33:11

Giving within the process of manifestation requires you to give without conditions or expectations. There are no strings attached, no hidden agendas. You just simply give. It does not matter what you give or how much you give; what matters is that you give consistently. Become a giving person. Go beyond the expectation to give only once or twice a year. Give unconditionally from the heart. In doing so, you will experience greater freedom and enjoyment of life.

> Continually give, continually gain.
>
> -Chinese proverb

Ellen Peterson

Chapter 11

# Of Course!
## The Dawning of Your Dreams Coming True

The tissue of life to be
We weave with colors all our own,
And in the field of destiny
We reap as we have sown.

John Greenleaf Whittier

It has been a long and difficult journey. You have dramatically altered the way you think, feel, and behave. You may still catch yourself at times saying something negative, but you are aware and able to turn it around quickly.

> Jane and Kathy were facilitating a weekend retreat. Jane was concerned that there would not be enough participants. Jane asked Kathy, "What would be the minimum number of people that you would do the retreat with?" Kathy responded, "I never thought about

a minimum number. The maximum number would be ten."

You are gradually surrendering such debilitating statements as "I can't afford" and "I'll never make it on time." You are beginning to trust that your needs will be met, and therefore can anticipate the good rather than the bad. Your daily thoughts, words, and actions are becoming more consistent with your dreams and desires. Alas, your dreams and desires can now make their way to you. This is a time of excitement and celebration.

Your view of the world has been changing steadily since opening this book. Things are noticeably different. You feel different. You smile more. You laugh more. You notice a change in you. Congratulations! Life is now beginning to flow in the direction that you have wanted it to flow. It is flowing toward abundance and away from lack and limitation. You are now experiencing firsthand the power of your own mind. It is fun. It is surprising. It is even amazing.

*You are in the flow of abundance.*

Being in the flow of abundance means that you are consistently mani-festing what you need in your everyday life: a pillow is on the hammock when you go to take your Sunday nap; a needed form is in your briefcase; there is a pen in your car when you get to the bank drive-thru; there are just enough stamps to mail your bills. Things are there for you. Simple and extraordinary things happen. After all, "with God all things are possible." With this change in your beliefs, you arrive on time, the meeting you forgot about was rescheduled, you were surprised to find ten dollars in your wallet, the door was unlocked, and your luggage arrived just in time. When you truly trust that all your needs will be met, you attract all the things you need or desire. All is well in your life, all the time.

Delores and Randy had tickets to a local theater production. They decided to have a nice dinner before the show, which started at 8:00 p.m. While at the restaurant, they sat enjoying one another's conversation for some time. Suddenly Delores glanced at her watch and noticed that they had only fifteen minutes until the start of the play. They both became anxious, as their meals had not yet been served. "What do we do?" they asked each other. Randy stated, "Once the doors to the theater are closed, they will not let us in." Within minutes, the waiter brought their meals to the table. They decided to eat quickly. Randy continued to panic, as he had been looking forward to this play. Delores instructed him to get the car while she waited for the bill, and reassured him that everything would be okay. She paid the bill and met Randy in the car. While driving to the theater, Delores continued to affirm that things would work out fine. They walked through the doors of the theater at 8:02 p.m. A woman greeted them and asked them for their names. As they gave their names, the woman responded, "Great, then we are all here." Delores and Randy took their seats and enjoyed the show. All was fine, just as Delores had affirmed all along.

*Good comes to those who wait (and trust).*

There are times when you must wait for your desired good to arrive. You are forced to wait for a letter to arrive in the mail or for an appointment to become available. This is the waiting period of manifestation. This is also the time when you may face the familiar feelings of frustration and discouragement. You become impatient when waiting for your good. You convince yourself that you have done everything possible, and still nothing has happened. You begin to doubt. You feel defeated. You convince yourself that what you want will never happen. Consequently, you choose to give up, just as you near the finish line. You grow tired of trying. You tell yourself that you are not going to win the race. You hear yourself say "Forget it" and "Why bother?" You certainly still want to win the race, but your thoughts are now of failure and defeat. It is in the waiting time of manifestation that you must push yourself across the finish line or drown in self-pity. This is the time when you need that final thrust of energy and motivation. Do not allow discouragement and defeat to throw you off course now. Choose instead to reframe your thoughts. Find the positive. Push forward. You can do it. The rewards are just within your reach.

It is easy to feel discouraged when your good is delayed. Many different factors can contribute to a delay. Your good can be delayed because of not using all the tools of prosperity described in these chapters. As you become more aware and conscious of the flow of abundance, you will more readily notice when your abundance is blocked. The washing machine breaks down. The check did not clear the bank. The dog is sick. The plans were cancelled. Experiences such as these remind you to review the tools of manifestation. Occasionally, you may lose focus and step out of the flow of abundance.

Have you written a gratitude list lately?

Have you been saying things that you do not really want to have happen?

Have you given in to fear or discouragement?

Have you given up and convinced yourself that your dreams will not come true?

It is so easy to step out of the flow of abundance. Do not despair. Do not give up. Choose to reevaluate instead. Something may indeed be contradicting your desired good. Evaluate your thoughts, words, feelings, and actions. Review the tools of manifestation and step back into the flow of abundance.

The delay of your good can also be related to "divine timing." That is, your good arrives with timing determined by the Universe. The Universe knows what is best for you. It also knows when you need what you need. Problems arise because you want immediate gratification. You would rather not have to wait. This is evident in every aspect of life, from fast food service to electronic filing of your taxes.

We constantly tell children that they must wait, yet as adults we do whatever we can to avoid waiting. We simply do not want to wait for anything. We now use credit cards at the gas pumps, so we do not have to be inconvenienced with going inside and waiting to pay. We are gradually eliminating the need to wait. We are accustomed to getting what we want immediately, and therefore we become more impatient and frustrated when our good is not delivered right away. We have lost sight of the significance of waiting.

Waiting provides you with the opportunity to observe rather than simply react. It gives you a greater appreciation of whatever you are waiting for. You appreciate the car for which you had to save money to purchase. You appreciate the home that you waited months to build.

So, wait your turn. Wait in line. As you learned as a child, "Give others a turn." Let others go before you. Accept the fact that you share this life with others. There are other cars on the road, and other people in the store and at the car wash. Learn to wait. In doing so, you demonstrate your ability to trust. There is enough time. You, too, will get your needs met.

It is also possible for good to arrive in an unexpected form. You expect your desired good to look and be a certain way, and yet the Universe delivers it in a different box. It is still your good. However, you tend to ignore or discount this good because it came in a different form. For instance, you expected money and instead received a tenant for your vacant apartment. Instead of recognizing your good in this alternate form, you continue to feel discouraged that the money has not yet arrived. You were simply looking elsewhere and missed the arrival of your good. Your good arrives at some point and in some way. It is your gift from the Universe. However, you must recognize it for the good that it is. Embrace all good.

Abundance continually flows from you and to you. Abundance is a birthright. We are all equally entitled to a life of abundance. As a child of God, you are entitled to the infinite riches of this life.

*Embrace your abundance*

Abundance is energy. It simply exists around you, but you need to know how to access it and use it to your advantage. It is just as easy to connect with abundance as it is to push abundance away. We chase it away when we fail to recognize it. We push it away when we focus on lack and limitation. We ignore our personal abundance when we think others have more than we do or when we feel that we simply do not have enough. We believe that our needs will not be met. We think that things will go wrong rather than right. The truth is that there are good things happening in your life every day. However, it is up to you to see these things as good.

*The good in life is not limited.*

God creates with abundance. When it rains, there are an infinite number of raindrops. We are not likely to sit down and count how many there are and wonder if there will be enough. The Universe constantly provides you with abundance. Look at the sand on the beach. Look at the skyscrapers. God does things in big ways, in infinite ways, which cannot be easily measured. This is also true of your life. It is filled with an unlimited supply of good things.

Like the ocean, your good has no limits. Yet you do not necessarily have to have the entire ocean to be fulfilled. You can take your abundance one wave on the shore at a time, knowing, of course, that there will always be more to follow. It is possible to take what you need and go back for more. It is not necessary to take it all at once. Take it a little at a time. Take as much as you need and return for more. Your good flows readily into your life.

As you consistently use the tools of manifestation, you will only expect good things in your life. You will gratefully embrace the "everyday miracles." Miracles are perceived as extraordinary events occurring in ordinary situations, but you experience many miracles in your everyday life. Everyday miracles are those events and experiences that occur on a regular basis yet cause you to feel amazed and surprised. For instance, you were just thinking of calling a friend and the telephone rings and it is that friend. You respond in amazement, "Wow, I can't believe that happened." Everyday miracles are simply when things are going "your way" or as you need them to go. There is no line at the bank when you are running behind schedule. There is a snow day when you did not have time to prepare for a meeting at work. The things that you need are on sale at the store.

Recognize and appreciate the everyday miracles of your life. Experience how easily the good flows into your life and affairs. In doing so, you will find yourself responding with confirmation rather than amazement. You now respond with "Of course" rather than "Amazing." Reactions of pure shock and amazement are reserved for those who truly do not believe in or use the tools of manifestation. You know different. You know that you are always cared for. Therefore, you find yourself chuckling when the good arrives, but it is no longer surprising.

> Beth had arrived at the gym but had forgotten a lock for the locker. She questioned whether she should still work out, but quickly decided that her needs would somehow be met. As she walked into the locker room, there on a bench was an abandoned gym locker with a key. She thanked the Universe.

It is important to recognize that manifesting your good is indeed a process. It does not happen immediately, nor does it happen at once. It happens because of what you are doing, saying, feeling, and believing.

Manifesting your dreams is a process like that of going to the McDonald's drive-thru for fast food. It is not possible for you to bypass the process, show up at the window, and expect to be given a double cheeseburger. There is a process that you must go through to receive your desired good. You must first identify what you desire, then you verbalize what you desire (also called *ordering).* Next, you wait your turn until you can give something (money) in exchange for your desire. Upon completion of all these steps, you manifest your desire and receive your good (double cheeseburger).

The manifestation of your good is dependent upon using all the principles of prosperity. Therefore, it is necessary for you to pay close attention to what you are thinking, feeling, and doing always. Manifestation requires you to be mindful and conscious of your thoughts and feelings. They must be consistent with what you want to manifest. Rely on the fact that all good comes your way. Do not settle for anything different. When the dishwasher breaks, affirm that it will be easily fixed and with little expense. Avoid saying, "Oh great, now we are going to have to buy a new one." Again, affirm only what you want to have happen.

*Always affirm that your good is on its way.*

Even if your desired good is delayed, continue to affirm that it is on its way. Remind yourself that it is in route to you. Do not send it back with your negative thoughts and feelings. Instead, continue to prepare for its arrival. Be ready. Make a place for it. It is still coming. It is not possible to lose your good. It is Divine good. It is intended for you to have and to experience. It is there for the taking. You simply need to know how to pick it up. Manifesting good in your life is an art. It requires the development of a skill. However, it is a skill that we all possess. We have just neglected to use it at times.

Barbara wanted to get a soda out of a hotel vending machine. She put her money into the machine, but the money kept dropping down and returning to her. Consequently, she believed that the machine was broken and that it would not be possible for her to get a soda. Her friend Karen, on the other hand, believed that Barbara could still get a soda, so she went over to the machine and asked Barbara what kind of soda she wanted. Karen then pressed the desired button. The soda dropped down, even though the machine had not taken any money.

*Manifesting good things begins with the knowledge that you always have what you need.*

The process of manifestation requires the consistent belief that your needs are always met. You always have what you need. This is true in every aspect of your life. The plane is on time. The car started. There was still time left on the meter. The checkbook was in the car. The sun shone on your wedding day. You already had a gift for an unexpected birthday. You were there during the family emergency. There were just enough eggs to make the cake. The house was clean when your cousin made a surprise visit. A client cancelled on the same morning your daughter came down with the flu. The grocery bill totaled the cash you had on hand. "Of course." These are everyday miracles. These are the things you needed to have happen, and therefore they happened. You live in abundance.

> I have learned in whatever situation I find myself, to be self-sufficient. I know indeed how to live in humble circumstances; I know also how to live with abundance. In every circumstance and in all things, I have learned the secret of being well fed and of going hungry, of living in abundance and of being in need. I have the strength for everything through Him who empowers me.
>
> --Philippians 4:11-13

# Chapter 12

# The Steady Flow of Abundance

It's kind of fun to do the impossible.

—Walt Disney

Life is good. And now comes the familiar question, "Can something so good really last?" The answer, of course, is yes. However, it will take a continued commitment on your part to stay in the flow of abundance. Staying in the flow of abundance always requires your conscious awareness and full attention. It is not possible to look the other way and think that the flow of abundance will somehow maintain itself.

Maintain your commitment to the process of manifesting your desires. The steady flow of abundance is maintained with the consistent use of the tools of manifestation. It is too easy to slip off the track. You must always be present to win. There is more to life than the routine of getting up in the morning, rushing to work, picking up groceries, putting gas in the car, and starting all over again tomorrow. Life is more than what is accomplished on automatic pilot. You are responsible for the fulfillment of your dreams and desires. Be aware and attentive to your life. Be an active participant in the experiences of your life. Live life consciously.

Staying in the flow of good requires commitment
and conscious awareness.

Staying in the flow of abundance requires focus. It requires attention to the details. The flow of energy already exists and therefore requires you to move into it and join with it. Take for example the way in which you merge your car onto a busy highway. Focus is necessary to merge with the pace already established by the other vehicles. Traveling at either a faster rate or a significantly slower rate creates a potentially dangerous situation. In addition, if you hesitate to merge with traffic, others are prevented from moving as well. Abundance in your life works the same way.

Beyond the need to pay close attention lies the need to surrender the fear and other feelings that tend to get in your way. Moving into abundance requires movement on your part. Become a master dreamer who makes his or her dreams a reality. Establish a comfortable pace that allows you to continue to move forward with your dreams. It is not necessary to "keep up with the Jones'" You simply need to keep moving forward while avoiding the emotional potholes. Stay alert and focused, lest you fall aimlessly into undesirable situations. Be aware of the important matters in your life. Surround yourself and your life with all that is positive and affirming. Merge with the flow of abundance that already exists for you.

*Life is not to be controlled, but to be experienced.*

Choose a life of ease rather than struggle. Swim with the current of life as opposed to battling your way through it. You have a greater chance of capsizing when you are fearful and untrusting of life and its varied circumstances. Surrender the need to control. Your reactions to life circumstances are a distinct measure of whether your life is ruled by fear or trust. Release the need to know what will happen next. Observe rather than react. Be strong enough to bend. Be trustful that what is intended to happen will indeed happen. Take the passenger seat some-times, buckle up for safety, and trust the outcome.

Trust that your needs will always be met. Trust will create a noticeable difference in your life. When you believe that your needs will be met, you worry less, you are more patient with others, you allow others to go first. You observe more and react less. Trust brings calmness. You catch yourself smiling and laughing more. People will enjoy your company, and hope that your view of life is contagious.

Establish and maintain a consistent relationship with your spiritual connection. Develop a means through which you can consistently connect with the Divine Source of your good. Your Higher Power is always at the door, knocking to come in. Answer the door! Do not ignore such life-enhancing opportunities. Spirituality is necessary for manifesting and maintaining a steady flow of abundance. It is necessary to believe in the Divine to be able to trust that something greater is at the driving wheel of your life. It is only then that you can permit yourself to let go of the struggle. Be willing to be divinely guided and cared for.

Surrender the fear that alienates you from others. Allow others to love you and to be close to you. Do not bear the burdens of life alone. That is merely a choice that you make. Share your burden with your Higher Power. Ask others for help. Avoid feeling like you need to be a martyr or prove to others how strong you are. Life is not meant to be a struggle. The trophy rarely goes to the person who endures the most pain. Instead, we tend to admire the person who succeeds without struggle, who makes life look easy.

Maintain a positive attitude about life, about yourself, and about your affairs. What you think will happen, will eventually happen. Pessimistic thoughts only sabotage you and hold your dreams at bay. Choose the positive rather than the negative. Your attitude holds the key to your abundance.

*Choose your words carefully.*

Ask for what you desire. Be clear in your intentions and do not compromise your truest desires. In other words, do not settle for less than what you genuinely want. Be mindful that God is listening. Do not give confusing messages or intentions. Do not change plans simply because something else came along. If your desire is to be self-employed, do not settle for working for someone else "in the meantime." In this way, you are accommodating fear rather than embracing trust. Believe in your dreams. Stay on course.

Make your words and actions congruent with your desires. Avoid negative language. Avoid phrases such as "I quit," "I can't do this anymore," and "I'm sick and tired of this." Avoid words that contradict and sabotage your dreams. Choose words that truly reflect your desires. Avoid the temptation to complain or criticize. Focus only on what you want to have happen.

*Stay in your integrity.*

Maintain your commitment to do what is right, what is honest, and what is fair. Be honest in all your affairs. Be honest in your interactions with others. Speak the truth. Do what you know is the right thing to do, no matter how uncomfortable or inconvenient it may be for you. Integrity affects the flow of abundance. Integrity and attitude are the gatekeepers of the flow of abundance. If your integrity and attitude are in place, the gate is open, and the flow is steady. If they are not in place, the gate is swiftly closed, and the flow is disrupted.

*Keep your affairs and your life in order.*

Clear away clutter and maintain room for your desired good. Create and maintain order in your life. Your emotional well-being is tied to your physical surroundings. Create the room and the space for feeling good about yourself and all matters important in your life. Creating order is just another way in which action creates abundance.

*Know your priorities.*

Put the people in your life first. Rarely do we regret not spending more time at work. Let your heart and not your wallet rule your life. Do not make decisions based solely on your finances. Money is not meant to have that degree of power over your life.

> The snow was falling consistently for many hours. Announcements were made via radio that the area schools were closed. The roads had not yet been plowed. The children awoke with excitement at the prospect of a fun-filled day, which was unplanned. The parents, on the other hand, were filled with worry and concern trying to figure out how they would get to work, and who would be available to watch their children. They felt inconvenienced by Mother Nature.

Loved ones are important to the quality of life, yet it is too easy to put money before our loved ones. "I can't afford to take the time off." This again relates to those beliefs of lack and limitation. There is a fear that there is not enough time. In this way, we choose to postpone enjoyment until it is more convenient for us. Yet most employers give time off to their employees. There is time for illness, family emergencies, and family deaths. We manage to take time off when we are devastated, but we cannot take time off when we are enjoying life.

> Janet's father-in-law had been sick with a heart condition for several months. He lived in another state. For weeks, when trying to make plans, Jane would often tell others, "It all depends on what happens with Dad." Due to the severity of the illness, she and her family knew that death was a possibility. When her father-in-law died, she stated, "This really isn't a suitable time. The kids have exams. Things are busy at work. And now I must cancel everything."

Be patient with yourself, as well as with others. Impatience is merely the uneasiness within you that you project onto others. Do not rush life. Life is to be savored and enjoyed.

## Live in the moment.

Observe the beauty of life. Notice the blossoming trees in spring. Notice the ant on the sidewalk and take time to watch it—it may have something to teach you. Watch the sunrise. Watch the sunset. Lay in a hammock. Send a card or note to a dear friend. Tell your children, your parents, your spouse, "I love you."

Say hello to the person in the elevator and on the sidewalk. There is no harm in being nice. It is a way in which you stay conscious of your life. Do not ignore, avoid, or hide from others. Be visible; be seen. Come out from behind the shadows of fear and embrace the light of day. It feels good.

## Live in gratitude.

Staying in abundance requires gratitude. Be grateful for the generous good in your life at the present time. Appreciate your life and the people who share it with you. Say thank you to the One who continually provides you with all that you need. Keep your good flowing with a grateful heart. When you feel your good slipping from you, take the time to write a gratitude list. The gratitude list will put you back in the flow of abundance.

## Commit to your dreams.

Stay committed to your desires. Do not give in to discouragement simply because your dreams are not manifesting fast enough. These are your dreams, and therefore they are worth your persistence. The only dreams that come true are those that are never surrendered. Remember the many actors, songwriters, musicians, and performers who started with nothing and ended up with everything. Persistence brings abundance. Therefore, nurture and honor your dreams. Protect them from the criticism or disapproval of others. Your dreams do not have to match or agree with the dreams and aspirations of others. You are the rightful owner of your dreams. They eagerly await your claim.

Allow the gift of the dream catcher to remind you of the possibility of using simple methods to manifest dreams. The dream catcher was introduced by the Native Americans and continues to be a valuable ornament for enhancing the dream world. The dream catcher is a simple, handcrafted web that is adorned with beads and feathers, and it usually hangs in a window. Its purpose is to catch bad dreams while filtering through the sweet and wonderful dreams. Simply hang this ornament in a window and believe in its magic. You should create an imaginary dream catcher, and safely store it in the deepest part of your heart. Let this dream catcher assist you in warding off the negative thoughts and feelings that sabotage the manifestation of your dreams. Believe in your dreams. Know that you deserve to make your dreams a reality. It is time to fully catch and embrace your hopes, dreams, and desires.

Keep a clear image of your dream catcher in your meditations and during quiet, serene moments. See and experience your dreams manifesting in a physical form. Use the tools of manifestation to maintain the steady flow of good and abundance in your life. Live your life fully. Make the most of life's many experiences. Fill each day with love and joy. Spend time with family. Be kind to others. Be kind to yourself. In doing so, you cannot avoid embracing prosperity and abundance. It is all within your reach. Abundance and prosperity are never-ending gifts to you. Shower yourself in abundance.

Choose Joy and Create Abundance!

# Appendix

The pages that follow offer you the opportunity to further explore the obstacles to your prosperity and guide you in the direction of manifesting your desires.

The form titled Acknowledging My Fears allows you to identify your fears. Often, people are unaware of the fears that hold them back from achieving their dreams. This simple checklist allows you to delve into your fears so you can understand them and heal them. There is also space for you to further explore your fears and how they originated in your life.

The Attitude Assessment is a series of completion statements that aid in identifying your inherited and current beliefs about money, time, and relationships. Develop an attitude of prosperity and begin manifesting your desires.

The Integrity Checklist, developed by the Wellness Institute, is a tool for aligning your life with good integrity. It provides you with a greater understanding of the depths of integrity and the ease with which you can step out of your integrity. The Integrity Checklist is an ongoing process. It is not intended to overwhelm you or convince you that your life must always be in meticulous order. Instead, it serves as a guidepost to help you move toward an uncluttered and uncomplicated life. It encourages you to finish the loose ends of your life to keep the path to prosperity free and clear. The Integrity Checklist is a tool that could be used regularly to assess your integrity and increase your understanding of this powerful block to prosperity.

There is a Personal Affirmations page included for you to write down your affirmations for easy reference. Chapter 7 provided you with instruction on how to create powerful affirmations. This is a place for you to write them down. Affirmations are powerful in the process of manifesting your dreams. Remember to say your affirmations daily.

The Personal Goals and Desires form gives you a designated place to write down your goals and desires. A goal that is written down is more likely to manifest than a goal maintained in the mind. This page is divided into personal and professional goals, but you may discover that you only have personal goals at this time. Revise the page as needed to fit your goals. Prioritize your goals and number them in order of importance to you. Include a completion date even if you feel unsure of an actual date. These are your goals. They deserve to be accomplished.

The last page of the appendix is a Gratitude List. On this page, write down all the things for which you are grateful in your life. Gratitude is the attitude for abundance and prosperity. The space is provided here. All you need to do is supply the time.

# Acknowledging My Fears

Check any of the following fears that you currently experience in your life:

| | |
|---|---|
| fear of being harmed | fear of being alone |
| fear of being manipulated | fear of being humiliated |
| fear of being rejected | fear of getting attention |
| fear of what others may | fear of being left/ |
| think | abandoned |
| fear of how others see me | fear that your needs will not |
| | be met |
| fear of acting "stupid" | fear of death |
| fear of being startled | fear of something bad happening |

Other fears:

Write about these fears and how they originated in your life:

# Attitude Assessment

*You can also use the same statements to identify your beliefs about time, relationships, and so on.*

1. As a child, I grew up believing that money:

2. The childhood messages that I received about money were:

3. My parents perceived/used money as:

4. Money was:

5. My current thoughts/feelings about money are:

6. Money affects my life in the following ways:

7. I need to:

# Integrity Checklist

Integrity is being honest and forthright with yourself and others. It is the foundation for success and prosperity. Complete the enclosed checklist. Make a commitment to yourself to complete tasks that interfere with your integrity. To stay in your integrity, review and update the list on a regular basis.

Date

I now agree to complete this Integrity Checklist by _____ (date) so that I can experience healthy control in my life and affairs.

To Do                                        Completion Date

A. Deliver any outstanding communications

      1. Letters to be written

      2. Acknowledgments

         To be given

         To be received

      3. Withheld thoughts/feelings to be        communicated

      4. Broken promises to be acknowledged and/or renegotiated

      5. Lies to be cleaned up

      6. Hidden/withheld information

B. Resolve any broken agreements

Ellen Peterson

To Do                           Completion Date

C. Resolve any upsets in your space

   (Clean it up or get rid of it)

D. Clean your living space totally

E. Clean your car/boat thoroughly

F. Clean your office space

G. Clean out and organize your personal files

H. Complete/schedule tasks on your desk

I. Fix or get rid of anything that does not work

J. Throw or give away what you no longer use or wear

K. Balance your checkbook

L. Pay your bills on time or make new arrangements with
   creditors

M. Organize your financial records/put them in order

N. Pay any taxes due and bring tax information up to date

O. Clean out your wallet/purse

P. Collect money owed

Q. Pay money owed

R. Handle/prepare a plan to address anything that impedes
   your physical/emotional/spiritual functioning
            (Resentments, alcohol/drug use or abuse)
S. Acknowledge any regrets and unspoken truths

T. Resolve any broken agreements with social institutions
            (Traffic tickets, overdue library books, misc. charges)

U. Other things I need to get honest about

# Appendix 4

## Personal Affirmations

Appendix 5

# Personal Goals And Desires

| Priority | Goals | Action Steps | Completion Date |
|----------|-------|--------------|-----------------|

Appendix 6

# Gratitude List

# Suggested Reading

Breathnach, S. B. *Simple Abundance: A Daybook of Comfort and Joy.*
New York: Warner Books, 1995.

Carlson, R. *Don't Worry, Make Money: Spiritual and Practical Ways to
Create Abundance and More Fun in Your Life.* New York:
Hyperion, 1991.

Choquette, S. Your *Heart's Desire: Instructions for Creating the Life* You
*Really Want.*
New York: Three Rivers Press, 1997.

Dominguez, J., and V. Robin. Your *Money or Your Life: Transforming
Your Relationship with Money and Achieving Financial
Independence.* New York: Penguin Books, 1991.

Dyer, W. W *Manifest Your Destiny: The 9 Spiritual Principles for Getting
Everything You Want.* New York: Harper Collins, 1997.

Gwain, S. *Creative Visualization: Use the Power of* Your *Imagination to
Create What You Want* in Your *Life.* California: Nataraj
Publishing, 1995.

Hay, L. *Heal Your Body: The Mental Causes for Physical Illness and the
Metaphysical Way to Overcome Them.* California: Hay House,
1982.

Hill, N. *Think* and Grow *Rich.* New York: Ballentine Publishing, 1960.

Maslow, A. *Toward a Psychology of Being.* Third edition. New' York: J.
Wiley & Sons, Inc., 1999.

Mundis, J. *How to Get Out of Debt, Stay Out of Debt & Live Prosperously.*
New York: Bantam Books, 1988.

Orman, S. *The 9 Steps to Financial Freedom: Practical & Spiritual Steps So You Can Stop Worrying.* New York: Crown Publishers, Inc., 1997.

Peterson, E. *Paid in Full: Freedom from Emotional and Financial Indebtedness.* CreateSpace Independent Publishing Platform. 2017.

Ponder, C. *Open* Your *Mind to Prosperity.* California: DeVorss Publications, 1971.

*The Dynamic Laws of Prosperity.* California: DeVorss Publications, 1985.

Ruiz, D. M. The Four Agreements: A Toltec Wisdom Book. California: Amber-Alien Publishing, 1997.

Webster's Unabridged Deluxe Dictionary. Second edition. Simon & Schuster, 1979.

Wilkinson, B. *The Prayer of Jabez: Breaking through to the Blessed Life.* Oregon: Multnomah Publishers, 2000.

# About the Author

Ellen Peterson, AKA *The Joy Therapist*, is a licensed and certified social worker and certified hypnotherapist who has counseled individuals, couples, and groups for more than thirty years. She offers simple and profound insights to yield positive life changes. Her unique ability to bring subconscious knowledge to the surface helps people move beyond the obstacles in life to greater joy and fulfillment. Her Personal Growth Programs offer profound life affirming experiences that enhance the lives of participants. She is the owner of Avenues Counseling Center in Ithaca, New York and has clients throughout the United States who seek her knowledge and expertise for emotional healing. For further information on Ellen Peterson and her influential work, visit www.EllenPeterson.com

# Paid in Full

Freedom from Emotional and Financial Indebtedness

Ellen Peterson

Paid in Full is an insightful book that assists its readers in understanding and resolving financial indebtedness, as well as emotional indebtedness. Stop being indebted to others in the form of money or guilt and enjoy the freedom that you deserve.

# Looking for more ways to

# Live Life Fully?

Visit www.EllenPeterson.com

Weekend Retreat Programs

Guided Meditations

Life Coaching

Made in the USA
Columbia, SC
19 September 2024

42621874R00109